D0174699

COMIC
INSIGHTS
The Art of Stand-up Comedy

COMIC
INSIGHTS
The Art of Stand-up Comedy

LOUIE ANDERSON   ROSEANNE
RICHARD BELZER   PAUL REISER
ELAYNE BOOSLER   CHRIS ROCK
GEORGE CARLIN   JERRY SEINFELD
ELLEN DEGENERES   GARRY SHANDLING
RICH JENI   SINBAD
JAY LENO   GEORGE WALLACE
RICHARD LEWIS   JONATHAN WINTERS
BILL MAHER   **by Franklyn Ajaye**

SILMAN-JAMES PRESS   LOS ANGELES

First Edition
10 9 8 7 6 5 4 3 2 1

Library of Congress Cataloging-in-Publication Data

Ajaye, Franklyn.
Comic insights : the art of stand-up comedy / by Franklyn Ajaye.
p.   cm.
1. Stand-up comedy.
2. Comedians—United States—Interviews.
I. Title.
PN1969.C65 A39 2002   792.7028—dc21   2002066964

ISBN: 1-879505-54-1

Cover design by Wade Lageose for Lageose Design

Printed and bound in the United States of America

Silman-James Press
1181 Angelo Drive
Beverly Hills, CA 90210

To all the brave souls who step on stage to tell the truth and make people laugh.

CONTENTS

ACKNOWLEDGEMENTS

First I would like to thank Ms. Gwen Feldman of Silman-James for publishing this book. It was just a strange quirk of what I call mystical serendipity that allowed this to happen. I had tried unsuccessfully to get this book published in the U.S. and kept getting rejected by publishers who felt that a book about the craft of stand-up comedy didn't appeal to a large enough market. So what had been a labor of love seemed destined to stay just that. However, while in Sydney, Australia, working at the Sydney International Comedy Festival, I happened to walk into Cinestore, a now defunct store that specializes in American television and film scripts and books about the performing arts. I saw a copy of the Silman-James book *Actors Turned Directors* which consisted of interviews of film and television directors. I looked through it, realized its similarity to what I had done, got the fax and phone number from international directory assistance, contacted Gwen at Silman-James, and here we are.

I would like to thank each and everyone interviewed for their candor and patience—as they all spoke very openly and thoroughly about their methodologies, philosophies, and craft. Not once did these very successful and busy people ever make me feel rushed. They gave me as much time as I needed to complete the interviews and every one of them left the door open for me to come back if I felt the need to. Needless to say, when dealing with people this busy and in such demand, this book would not have been possible without the tremendous help given me by their representatives and assistants. My sincere gratitude goes to Shelly Ondrush, Geoff Abrams, Arthur Spivak, George Shapiro, Rob Wilner, Arthur Imparato, and

Michael Green for their help in contacting many of the comedians. And I give special thanks to Ms. Ronnie Rubin for goading me into teaching a class at UCLA, which then gave me the idea for the book; to Mr. Greg Amerson of HBO, who was invaluable in getting me the tapes of many of the comedians' HBO specials so that I could study them and prepare the areas that I wanted to explore; and to Peter Glassberg and Valerie Cole for transcribing many of the interviews. I would like to also give deep thanks and appreciation to my manager and friend, Mr. Ben Hill, who always encouraged me in this endeavor.

INTRODUCTION

In October of 1971, I made my stand-up comedy debut on an "amateur night" at The Village Gate, a renowned jazz club on Bleecker Street in Greenwich Village. I was a floundering first-year student at Columbia Law School in New York who had been encouraged by all my friends to try my hand at stand-up comedy. It's easy to flounder in law school when you're not going to class or doing any of the reading. Basically, I would drop by the school to get a cup of their good coffee, then go back to my apartment to sleep. Not exactly the fast track to *Law and Order*. So with my younger brother Eric in tow for moral support, I stepped on a stage that night to do a five-minute spot—and bombed. Not one laugh. Those five minutes seemed like an hour. All I remember is a man with a crew cut and a stone face sitting in the front row.

Riding the subway back uptown that night I was crushed, and my comedy future looked so bleak to me that the next day I was sitting wide awake in my classes at Columbia. But after four more dry months of Torts, Contracts, and Civil Procedure, I felt I had a better chance of becoming a criminal than a lawyer and decided to risk dying on a comedy stage again. But not without giving my last disastrous appearance a great deal of thought. I had to figure out what had gone wrong—but more importantly, where to begin.

So I comedy "woodshedded" (i.e., started watching every stand-up comedian I could on television.) I'd watch *The Tonight Show* with Johnny Carson one night and *The Dick Cavett Show* the next. I'd study the different monologue styles and mannerisms of Carson and Cavett and do my own neophyte analysis, notebook in hand. I bought comedy albums and tapes and listened to them exhaustively trying to decipher what it took to be a funny and artistic stand-up comedian. Desire and desperation created discipline, as I tried to discover the key to my comedy essence for public consumption.

The next time I stepped on stage was March 14, 1972, at "Hoot Night" at The Bitter End in Greenwich Village, and I was significantly better. I got some decent laughs. Afterward, a man named Ted Lorenz (who was running the Hoot Night) said, "You've got a funny head, keep at it." That was all I needed to hear, and it gave me the confidence I needed to flunk all my law classes. By the time I realized that he was talking about the shape of my head, I had already left school.

Throughout my career, whenever I perform at a nightclub or college, I'm often approached after a show by someone interested in pursuing a career as a stand-up comedian. They're usually somewhat shy, hesitant, searching for any insight they can get. I recognize them, of course, because I recognize myself and all the insecurities I had when I was starting—waiting patiently outside the dressing room at the Troubadour for a chance to blurt out one question to Robert Klein, going to The Comedy Store night after night to watch Richard Pryor, talking to Bob Newhart at a clothing store I worked at—from shoe-level, as I measured him for a suit. I remember how confused I was, and how I thirsted for any bit of insight into the art of performing stand-up comedy. And yet each time I left the presence of those great comedians, I always felt vaguely dissatisfied, feeling as though I hadn't asked the right questions. And I hadn't, because I didn't know what to ask. Many years later, by the time I knew the questions, I'd already been forced to figure out the answers.

In 1992, while taking a class at the UCLA Class Extension Professional Studies Program in Sitcom Directing from then *Murphy Brown* director Peter Bonerz, I was approached by Ms. Ronnie Rubin, the head of the highly regarded program and asked if I would teach a class in stand-up comedy. At first I declined, unsure if I could communicate my personal and idiosyncratic method to someone else with a positive effect. But the more I thought about it, the more I became intrigued. I agreed to do it. Since I considered myself a classical monologist, I decided to call the class The Art of Stand-Up Monology. My intention was to show aspiring comedians how to tap into their natural comedic essence for material, and how that was most easily accomplished by adhering to one's individual point of view. I also had such other gifted stand-up monologists as George Carlin, Jerry Seinfeld, Sinbad, Elayne Boosler, Paul Reiser, and Ellen DeGeneres come and speak to the class about their own particular approach and methods. After each guest spoke, a brief question-and-answer session was conducted, which I augmented with questions of my own.

At the conclusion of the semester, each student performed a five-minute stand-up comedy monologue at The Improvisation comedy club in Los Angeles. Without fail, each student had improved significantly during the class in pulling humor out of their personal feelings and observations about life, and many were quite funny. But what was more interesting was watching that moment during the semester when each student discovered his or her true point of view as reflected in their routines. It was usually a defining moment in their comedy signifying growth and more laughter. Teaching them to explore their true feelings and thoughts had enabled them to bring their own point of view into focus, and to open a tunnel to their true sense of humor.

The comedians who influenced me—Richard Pryor, George Carlin, Robert Klein, Lenny Bruce, Dick Gregory, Bob Newhart, Bill Cosby, Woody Allen, and Mort Sahl—all had distinctive points of view as they elevated stand-up comedy, allowing it to take its place alongside jazz as one of the only two creative art forms indigenous to America. A distinctive point of view is what each of the comedians in this book possess in abundance, and it's what is missing from many of today's young comedians, causing them to blend into the comedy woodwork.

In addition to those comedians who spoke to my class, I interviewed a wide variety of other top stand-up comedians for this book—each who has his or her unique point of view and stand-up comedy style. From the austere writing-self-discipline of a Jerry Seinfeld to the gregarious spontaneity of a Sinbad to the neurotic, jazz-like riffs of a Richard Lewis, to the gentle observations of a Paul Reiser and Ellen DeGeneres to the blunt challenges to societal hypocrisy of a George Carlin, Chris Rock, Elayne Boosler, or Bill Maher, I've included a variety of approaches, philosophies, and working methods so that aspiring comedians can read this book, find the "method" for his or her own madness in the comedian whose comedic sensibility speaks to him or her, and use this influence to develop his or her own individual style. Consequently, aspiring comedians will have the advice of the best comedy role models available at their fingertips when trying to develop their own comic voice and career. They're all here.

I also interviewed agents, comedy-club owners, and a manager who specializes in comedians to get their insights on what they look for in a stand-up comedian.

I wrote this book to demystify the process of becoming a stand-up comedian without diminishing it. In talking to the other comedians for this book, an interesting thing happened to me— my own interest in performing stand-up comedy returned. Listening to these truly great comedians talk about their experiences and methods made me think again about all the things I'd once found interesting in stand-up: The little challenges and puzzles to be solved on a nightly basis. The chance to explore your thoughts and beliefs through your comedy, and discover their sometimes surprisingly true validity. And so I resumed performing stand-up comedy at the Melbourne International Comedy Festival in 1997. As I prepared for that intense and challenging six-night-a-week performance for the three-week "comedy boot camp" schedule, I found myself doing everything I've written about in this book. I went back to basics, the fundamentals— working on developing each of the elements of stand-up comedy. And it worked. And I still peruse the interviews from time to time for inspiration or to see how these great stand-ups approach a performance problem.

This is not a joke primer, but a philosophical approach to developing material that will help anybody who wants to be a comedian unlock his or her true comedic essence. That is, if you have one, which honestly not everybody does. And if that's the case, then it's best that you find that out too. But I'll do my best to help you answer that question by covering such subjects as how to properly study comedians, the elements of good stand-up comedy, developing your material, the role of the subconscious in creativity, using the "third eye," preparing for the first time on stage, as well as bombing and how to bounce back—along with other valuable information from the many tremendously funny and skilled comedians in this book that will help you to decrease your own comedic "trials and errors."

Part I

NOTES OF A JAZZ COMEDIAN ON STAND-UP

*I never thought it was hard to make people laugh.
In fact, when someone told me it was hard to make
people laugh, I laughed.*

—Jack Graiman (former comedian)

First Steps To Becoming a Stand-Up Comedian

Study The Good Ones

The first and most important step for anybody who wants to be a good stand-up comedian is to make sure that you watch the good ones and study them intently so that you can get a feel for *why* they're funny. You may think that's unnecessary advice, but when I taught my class, on the first day I asked each student to name his or her favorite comedian. They could all answer with no problem. But when I asked them what made that comedian so funny, they didn't have a clue. They'd invariably answer, "I don't know, they're just funny." That's not good enough. You have to be able to coolly appraise a comedian's techniques, strengths, and weaknesses to notice what works and doesn't work so that you can dispel any sense of awe and become more objective. Only then can you understand how they generate laughter, and thus apply their expertise to help you develop.

So what should you study in a comedian? You must study their deliveries, their use of their bodies, their timing, and their use of audio and vocal effects. Videotape their routines and play them back to see if you can understand the logic that got them to their punchlines. Even better, write down some of their best lines so that you can see how it looks on paper. That way your own routines and punchlines won't look so strange to you when you write them. A beneficial current development is that many of the top comedians

(Seinfeld, Rock, Reiser, Carlin, Sinbad, DeGeneres) have written humorous books, giving you a great opportunity to see their words and the way they think in print. In addition, many have released performance videos that you can rent and study at leisure, but I strongly suggest that you also listen to comedy CDs to discover how "good comedy" performs on many levels to make you laugh. When listening to a comedy album, you don't have any help from your eyes. Yet a good comedian can verbally paint a picture that taps into your imagination and creates a "visual" in your head. When I was starting out in 1972, I listened to the comedy albums of Woody Allen, George Carlin, Richard Pryor, Robert Klein, Lenny Bruce, and Bill Cosby as they used their comedic skills to create pictures and tap into our imaginations. This is the skill that you want to develop, and you'll find studying their comedy CDs invaluable.

Zero In On Your Sensibility

After you've started looking at comedians more analytically, the next step is to zero in on the comedian or comedians whose sense of humor and style of comedy reminds you of the sense of humor you naturally display around your friends and associates when you are relaxed. When you find the comedian who reminds you of what you do naturally, that particular comedian can serve as a guide or influence. In my case, even though I loved the comedy of Bill Cosby, Jonathan Winters, and Woody Allen, the comedians who seemed to embody what I seemed to be doing naturally among my friends were Richard Pryor, Robert Klein, and George Carlin. So I studied those three giants particularly hard. But I never tried to copy them in any way. Instead, I tried to isolate and incorporate elements of their approach in my own approach to writing and performing stand-up. The incisive truth and honesty of Richard Pryor, the offhand informality, conversational delivery, and restless societal probing of George Carlin, the college-educated vocabulary and iconoclastic viewpoint of Robert Klein—all of these were elements that I strove to have in my comedy. Trying to synthesize these various elements with my own interests and point of view enabled me to create an individual style.

If you've never told a joke or been funny around your friends, but you still want to become a stand-up comedian, you can find your own sense of humor by studying the comedian who consistently makes you laugh the most—that particular comedian is tapping into your comedic sensibility and helping you identify where your own sense of humor lies. This will be a great aid to helping you know the direction that you want to take your comedy material.

The Proper Use Of Influences

The greatest gift that I received from my main comedic influences (Richard Pryor, Robert Klein, and George Carlin) was their excellence at their craft. Seeing them always let me know how good I wanted to be, and how far I had to go. I remember watching Richard Pryor for a week at The Comedy Store in 1973 and leaving each night both awed and depressed. My material seemed so trivial compared to his—and I had my own comedy album out at the time. I kept looking at his head and saying to myself, "It's just a normal-sized head. How could all those ideas come out of a normal-sized head?" But seeing him perform at such a high skill level made me work harder to try and add more depth to my material. In fact, after I finished brooding, with vivid memories of his brilliance, I worked the next week in Houston and added physical movement to my act for the first time by walking back and forth along the stage. And more importantly, I started to act out the behavior of the high-school characters that I had previously only talked about, which improved my performance immensely. All because of seeing how Richard Pryor's acting added to his performance. A few years later at The Comedy Store, I watched Richard Pryor build his famous "Mudbone" routine literally from one line on Tuesday into a long, detailed routine by Saturday, which was the night he added the lines about "the Polar bear with the little tiny feet." What was particularly instructive to me was watching him add a little something to the bit each night, which meant that he was either listening to an audiotape or at least thinking a lot about this routine on a daily basis.

At the time I was starting out, I listened to every good comedy album I could. Though I knew nothing formally about stand-up comedy, I would write down my own observations in my own attempt to gain some insight into their art. The following is a twenty-year-old analysis I did of Bill Cosby after listening to his album *To Russell, My Brother Whom I Slept With*, an album I heartily recommend to anyone who wants to do long autobiographical routines and stories. Keep in mind that this was my own unschooled attempt to analyze what a top-flight comedian was doing. However, I can say unequivocally that this neophyte analysis helped me better understand all the things that a good stand-up comedian is doing when he or she is making you laugh.

Bill Cosby

1. Does sound effects (footsteps, doors, covers, bed crashing).

2. No jokes.

3. Lot of energy and animation.

4. Good voices.

5. Gives his point of view.

6. Does not try to go for absurd or bizarre lines, but lets humor come from situation.

7. Uses pauses and takes his time.

8. Does real-life situations from his life.

9. Gives characters attitudes.

I recently watched Bill Cosby's stand-up video *49* while in Melbourne, Australia, preparing for their comedy festival, and did another analysis of the master comedian to see what I could learn. It went as follows:

1. He gives human qualities (voices, thoughts, pride) to objects and body parts.

2. Lets the audience calm down after a long laugh before starting a new routine.

3. Very close observation of his own behavior during an event, which he recreates for the audience.

I used to also write down specific lines from George Carlin, Redd Foxx, and Cosby so that I could see them in print. Then I'd write an analysis as well. Here's an example that I did with lines by George Carlin and Redd Foxx.

George Carlin

1. "You can say, 'I pricked my finger,' but you can't say, 'I fingered my prick' in public."

   Analysis: An example of a reversal of a commonly used, everyday saying.

Redd Foxx

1. "I know that Jesus is black because you can't wear no hat for thirty years in the desert and stay white."

   Analysis: Example of a logical statement as an extension from given facts.

2. "Hire the handicapped. They're fun to watch."

   Analysis: Statement of a politically incorrect truth.

There's a big difference between imitating a comedian and being strongly influenced by one. As long as you have the concept of self-expression at the forefront of your mind, you will never be a carbon copy of your comedic influences. And when you take the various elements of a comedian or comedians that you admire and synthesize them with your individual viewpoint, you will create something new and original. When I went to Melbourne to perform in their comedy festival, I took along the Woody Allen tape *Stand-Up Comic* and Richard Pryor's CD *Craps After Hours* and listened to both of them during the days before the festival—along with watching the aforementioned Bill Cosby videotape—to reinforce in me the things that I wanted to put into my comedy. I found myself once again inspired by Woody Allen's ability to write such plausibly absurd stories with clarity, Richard Pryor's ability to inject a sense of theater and real and distinct-sounding characters into his stand-up, and Bill Cosby's inimitable ability to hold an extremely casual, humorous conversation with a large audience. But most importantly I admired all three's ability to take me into my imagination and create pictures in my head.

You can be influenced by artists other than comedians when it comes to the approach you want to take to your comedy as well. In my opinion, all the arts are related. My creative heroes when I was starting were Miles Davis, Richard Pryor, Marlon Brando, and François Truffaut as well as singer-songwriters like Bill Withers, Curtis Mayfield, Gil-Scott Heron, and Joni Mitchell. I was drawn to their continual creativity, and the fact that there was great depth and truth to their work. The lyrics of the singer-songwriters mentioned as well as those of Bob Dylan and James Taylor inspired me to try to add a social-commentary aspect to my material. My goal was to combine an everchanging, "jazzy," loose feel to my presentation with the verbal incisiveness of the best folk-rock lyrics. Whether I ultimately attained that or not is debatable—but though I had never communicated this goal to anyone, one night as I entered The Improv, I heard Bill Maher refer to me as, "the jazz comedian." So, as often as possible study, other art forms and artists (filmmakers, writers, musicians, painters, playwrights, actors, etc.), read what these top practitioners have to say about their approach to their art, and see if you can relate any of their insights to your own comedy.

SUMMARY

- ◆ Analytically study the best stand-up comedians through the use of videotapes, books, CDs, and cassettes.

- ◆ Zero in on the comedian whose sense of humor or style is reminiscent of the style of humor you display around your friends.

- ◆ If you've never been funny, zero in on the comedian whose humor you enjoy the most for insight into your own sense of humor.

- ◆ Isolate the comedic elements of your favorite comedian or comedians, then synthesize and incorporate these elements into your own presentation.

- ◆ Keep self-expression as your goal and as a protection against imitating your influences.

- ◆ All art is related, so you can use artists other than comedians to inspire your approach to your comedy.

The Elements Of Stand-Up Comedy

When we watch successful stand-up comedians, they seem to be just doing what comes naturally—being funny. To a certain extent that's true—many comedians have been funny people since they were kids. However, to be a professional comedian you have to be funny on demand, regardless of your emotional state. Raw innate ability is not enough to guarantee success on a regular basis. You can't just be "naturally funny" every night. Consequently, you have to develop techniques to compensate for those times when your talent or creative spark isn't there.

Stand-up comedy technique can be broken up into certain essential elements, some of which—but not all—are employed to some degree by every successful stand-up comedian. They are:

Point Of View/True Thoughts And Feelings

It all starts here. An individual point of view is by far the most important element for memorable stand-up comedy. It's what makes any artist of merit truly stand out. Artists as disparate as Picasso, Richard Pryor, Miles Davis, Woody Allen, The Beatles, Salvador Dali, Marlon Brando, Martin Scorcese, and Quentin Tarantino all have in common the fact that they possess very individualistic points of view through which they filtered their artistic perceptions of life.

Many great comedians will tell you that from a very early age people would laugh at the things that they said, even when they were serious. Why? Because their serious "take" or point of view struck the listener as funny or odd. Your point of view is the voice you hear when you talk to yourself. As a stand-up, tapping into how you really feel or think about this madness we call life is the key to tapping into your true sense of humor. We don't all look at life the same way, despite the best efforts of the media and politicians to paint us as a collective group that marches in some sort of intellectual goose-step. An aspiring comedian must be determined to get to his or her true feelings on a subject and convey that to the audience. Figure out what you're feeling or interested in because the goal is to get the audience interested in what you're interested in. Good stand-up comedy is drawing people into your head.

Another advantage of staying true to your point of view is that it offers good protection against having your material stolen—or at least it will moderate the damage. Not that people won't try, given the fact that, like any profession, the stand-up comedy world has its share of unscrupulous people devoid of originality. But it will make it tougher for them because your material will have a distinctive point of view. It won't just be jokes, but routines and situations from which jokes can't be taken out of place. The hacks can steal your joke, but they can't steal the way you look at life. So you may lose a few gems to the hacks, but you'll be able to come up with more gems because you'll still have your individual outlook. As you continue to perform, your routines and jokes will have the stamp of your "uniqueness." People will not only laugh at your material, they will be fascinated at the workings of your mind and look at the subjects you cover in a different way. Then when they think about that subject, they will think about what you said. Soon, they'll want your "take" on things, and eventually in their minds your material and point of view will become indelibly linked.

There's nothing more exciting than going on stage armed only with your observations on something or some form of seemingly obscure behavior, and having the audience erupt in laughter after you point out the previously unnoticed—but now abundantly obvious—absurdities. To have commitment to your point of view is one of the most difficult things to do especially if your initial attempts to get laughter don't get any. But you must be resolute. Originality is never embraced as quickly as the commonplace. Richard Pryor initially caught a lot of grief from the entertainment industry and audiences when he changed from the safe, suit-clad comic to the aggressively profane purveyor of the truth as he saw it. But he didn't waver. He stood behind his point of view. Sam Kinison used to clear a club with his angry tirades when he first started. Ditto for the late Bill Hicks. By the end, they were filling these same clubs with the same comedic approach. Roseanne's defiant adherence to her strong point of view on marriage and family life initially distinguished her stand-up act, and then lifted what could've been a stock, formulaic sitcom into an insightful exploration into the life of blue-collar American families.

Honesty

Noted author Frank Norris once said about his approach to his work, "I told them the truth. They liked it or they didn't like it. What had that to do with me? I told them the truth." That quotation sums up how I feel about the importance of honesty—an absolutely essential element that should be inextricably linked to your point of view. Don't try to give a funny opinion; give your opinion in a way that will be funny. Plant your feet, focus on the odd details of a situation that has caught your attention, and describe what you honestly see or feel. Is it exasperation, amusement, anger, disgust, anxiety, amazement? Try to tune into and identify your honest feelings—and express them.

Delivery

The delivery of a stand-up comedian is like the serve of a tennis player or the tee shot of a golfer. It's what starts the routine rolling to its humorous conclusion. A bad delivery can ruin the best joke.

Think of all the jokes people have told that died, causing them to utter the infamous line, "I guess you had to be there." "I guess I should have told it better" would be more accurate. What is a good delivery? Like that AE-1 camera commercial used to say, "It's so complex, it's simple." A good delivery is one that allows the audience to follow your train of thought. It is the bridge to the window of your thinking. A monologue is a one-way conversation that gives the illusion of being a dialogue. So you should focus on talking to the audience, not at the audience. They can detect when you're detached and just doing it in a rote fashion with no attempt to really connect with them.

Think of the audience as a giant individual whom you're trying to communicate with. The audience must be with you every step of the way if they're going to laugh when you get to the punchline. And it's the delivery that keeps the audience on track as you try to paint a picture in its collective mind. It can be fast or slow (though not too much of either), but it must contribute to the audience's understanding of where you eventually land. Since the audience will be strangers to you, they will be introduced to your way of looking at life for the first time. So, clarity and economy are paramount. By economy, I mean the ability to verbally elaborate with a minimum of words. Jerry Seinfeld and Ellen DeGeneres in particular have very clear, economical deliveries. With a few words they can give the audience all the information it needs to follow the twists and turns of their mind as they head to the punchline. By the same token, Paul Reiser has a more convoluted, idiosyncratic delivery, but the important words in his setup are always clearly spoken.

Timing

Good timing is an integral part of an effective delivery and relates in particular to two areas of a comedian's act: the delivery of the punchline and picking the right moment to start the next joke after the audience has laughed. Good timing is basically "good pauses." Jack Benny, that late, great master of timing and space, once said, "If I take the time to wait to tell them, those silences are as strong as the words."

Louie Anderson, who admits to being influenced by Jack Benny, has exquisite timing and gives "good pauses." He will build his story and just before he hits the punchline, he'll pause. This type of pause is effective because it gives the audience a moment to digest everything you've said up to that point and bring the whole picture into clear mental focus. This pause is the "lighting of the fuse." Then the punchline detonates the stored-up images in their imagination. When you take a pause before delivering your punchline, you will be using silence as a creative entity in itself, much as Miles Davis did with his music in the late fifties and early sixties. You must not be afraid of small bits of silence. To use it well is the height of confidence and skill for a comedian. It increases the tension in a good way and adds contrast like a curve ball complements the fastball of a good pitcher. Not even Nolan Ryan could throw smoke all the time and get away with it. He had to add a curve ball and change-up.

The second place where good timing is essential is when you've gotten a good laugh from the audience and have to decide when to start your next routine. Many inexperienced comedians just rush into their next routine, actually forcing the members of the audience to stop laughing quicker than they normally would. Don't make the audience keep putting brakes on their laughter. The constant starting and stopping gives an abrupt quality to your act. Let the laughter run its natural course. Then, before it drops into total silence, start the next routine. This way you build an almost musical rhythm that has its own natural ebbs and flows. If you cut off the audience continually in the middle of laughter, you actually run more of a chance of them getting laughed out. Whereas if you let the laughter die out on its own, the audience catches its breath and is able to laugh longer as the show goes on. I use this technique in order to add what I call my "afterthought" lines. Those are the additional line or thoughts that I come up with after delivering the original hard punchline to extend the humor. These lines are usually more subtle, and if I don't wait, the audience'll miss it.

Letting the laughter subside naturally is related to letting the laughter build on a cerebral joke that might take a while for the audience to get—or is gotten initially by only a few people. Of course, you can't wait forever for the audience to get the joke, but you should give them at least two seconds to join in before you go on to the next one. In time, you'll develop a feel and your timing will improve.

Visuals

When doing stand-up comedy, you should always think about adding visual elements to your performance. This can be done as simply as just walking back and forth across the stage—thus making the audience follow you with their eyes. Especially if you're a one-liner comedian, standing in one place can be deadly—particularly in these days of shrunken attention spans. Though, if you can write lines of the quality of a Steven Wright or a Dennis Miller, you can get away with standing in one spot. But if you can't, walking back and forth also helps by creating the illusion that you are thinking of the routines on the spot, giving your performance a more spontaneous feeling. And I've actually found that sometimes the act of pacing helps me think of ideas.

You can add the visual element in a more indepth manner by acting out the parts of the different people whom you talk about in your comedy. This fleshes out your scenes and gives them more dimension. I'm not talking about trying to turn yourself into a comedic Marlon Brando, just using your observational abilities to recreate the attitudes, facial expressions, and physical mannerisms of those you're trying to illuminate. Of course, this takes some acting ability, but doing this successfully will add a bit of "magic" to your act.

Audio Effects And Vocal Characterizations

Audio effects are tremendous enhancements to a stand-up comedian's performance and come in two forms: sound effects and vocal characterizations. The use of good sound effects in a stand-up's presentation adds tremendously, but it requires a special talent. Bill Cosby, Jonathan Winters, and Robin Williams are great at this. A sheet coming off a bed, an airplane engine, footsteps coming down the hall, a door opening—these are all sounds that they've used to help paint the picture. This is an optional element, not an absolute essential for your act. As I said, this requires a special talent, but if you can do this, add it to your arsenal. (For more on this see the Richard Jeni interview.)

Vocal characterizations are not as difficult—they just require a good ear and some skill at mimicry on your part. I'm not talking about full impressions like Rich Little does, but about creating voices just different enough from your own, and distinct enough to suggest the presence of other people in your routines or stories. In a sense, it puts more people on the stage to help you hold the audience's attention. Richard Pryor and Jonathan Winters were the best at it. Once again, this is an optional but extremely valuable element if you can develop it.

Concentration

Concentration or focus is what is needed to tie your performance all together. You can't just wing it; you have to have some type of plan for the show. You have to be focused on the task at hand—which is to make the audience laugh at your humorous observations. When you concentrate, it helps with your mental visualization, which frees your imagination. Before you know it, you're so involved in what you're thinking and talking about that you practically entertain yourself. Then the joy and vividness of what you are seeing is communicated to the audience, and your enjoyment becomes infectious.

When I'm on stage, not only am I thinking about the routine that I'm currently doing, but also where I want to be two routines down the line. I'm also taking note of how the audience is reacting to my current routine. If they're not reacting as I'd like, I have to start thinking of bailing out of it and changing directions from the related routines or subjects that I had planned for the show. I found that on the nights that I had trouble concentrating, the flow of the material would suffer and my performance would have a feeling of fits and starts. A performance can be a series of constant adjustments. And it all takes concentration. Your mind must be alert and focused. When your concentration suffers, the show suffers. It's an absolute equation.

Stage Presence

This is an intangible quality that is the combination of—or the sum of all—the previously mentioned elements. It is the way you "command your space" on stage. Many comedians think this means coming at the audience with rapid speech and an aggressive attitude. But that's not necessary. If you're soft-spoken or laid-back, a good delivery, good timing, a strong point of view, and the words "commitment and conviction" tattooed in your brain will help you create a strong stage presence.

When you walk on the stage, you are "going to war." Not always, of course, but this will certainly more often than not be the case in your early attempts to get a room of strangers to laugh. More so than any other art form, the stand-up comedian is involved in a power struggle with the audience. Ideally, you want to be in a fifty-fifty power-sharing arrangement with the audience—both of you there for a mutually enjoyable experience. And that is usually the case when you have established a national reputation with widespread acceptance. When you have a national reputation, you are "pre-sold" so to speak, so the audience that is coming to see you is automatically on your side and tuned into your point of view. But when you're just starting out, you'll have to face a number of people who are basically daring you to make them laugh.

Psychologically, you must be prepared to stand your ground in the midst of the silence detonating all around you. This can only come from you truly understanding your point of view and being committed to putting it out there for the audience to consider. The audience will sense that you're not intimidated—even if they're not laughing—and respect that you're in command of your space. Obviously the audience has veto power signified by whether they laugh or not, but you—not them—retain the ultimate power to decide what they're going to get the opportunity to laugh at.

Smooth Transitions

This is the ability to move your material from subject to subject on stage, all the while making seemingly unrelated subjects appear connected and blend into each other. Though to be honest, I don't think that most audiences care if the transitions between comedic subjects are smooth. However, if you can accomplish this, it will make your performance go faster in the audience's mind, and help weave a spell. Seamless transitions make your show flow like a river. A river with tributaries is how I think of my transition lines. A technique that I developed quite naturally to help me make smooth transitions was to use a word or phrase from the next routine in the preceding one. For example, I used to do a routine about black people not playing golf because they would never be caught dead in plaid pants. I would end it by saying, "Seeing black people in plaid pants would be some science-fiction stuff, like something you'd see on *Star Trek*." Then I would go into my *Star Trek* routine and the audience would not feel any abrupt transition between topics as they do when a comedian jumps around from subject to subject. In effect, I had announced the title of the next routine in the previous one, and subtly got the audience ready for the change of topic.

During my first week of performing at the Melbourne International Comedy Festival after a three-year performance layoff, I couldn't make the smooth transitions that I normally like to do, and while I was very aware of it, the audience wasn't put off at all by the somewhat-disjointed (by my standards) flow of my act, and gave me a great reaction. They weren't concerned, but I was. With increased stage time, I noticed my ability to make connections returning. For example, I did a routine on the judicial system in Iran where I have a guy being charged in an Iranian court with "Corruption on Earth," and I had his lawyer say, "Forget reasonable doubt, we've got to prove that you weren't on the planet." The lawyer then says the afterthought line, "I've got some old Heaven's Gate applications, maybe I can backdate them." I then went into a long routine on the religious suicide cult. That phrase "Heaven's Gate" allowed me to move the audience from the Middle East to the suicide cult in San Diego without them missing a beat. By the end of the second week of the festival, I got a great review that commented on the unique point of view and the smoothness (two vital comedy elements) of my act. Though I doubt the reviewer could trace that smoothness to the fact that I was making disparate routines flow into each other. So, look for phrase or word connections between routines for smooth transitions. This is an optional element, but it truly distinguishes the artist from the journeyman.

SUMMARY

Effective stand-up comedy technique consists of the following essential elements:

Point Of View

◆ Your individual point of view is the most important element in your comedy arsenal.

◆ Tap into your true thoughts or feelings on a subject and convey them to the audience.

◆ Unscrupulous comedians can steal your jokes, but they can't steal your point of view—which is what generates your material.

◆ You must be resolute with your point of view if it isn't initially accepted.

Honesty

◆ Don't try to give a funny opinion, give your opinion in a funny way.

◆ Focus on the details that you notice and tell the truth about what you see or feel.

Delivery

◆ A good delivery allows the audience to follow your train of thought.

◆ Your delivery can be fast or slow, but it must contribute to the audience's understanding of where you land—the punchline.

◆ Clarity and economy of words is paramount.

◆ Talk to the audience, not at them.

Timing

◆ "Light the fuse" to your joke by taking a pause before you deliver the punchline.

◆ When you get a good laugh from the audience, let it subside naturally before you start the next joke.

◆ Give the audience a few seconds to get a cerebral joke.

◆ Don't be afraid of silent moments.

Visuals

◆ Always think about adding a visual element to your performance if possible.

◆ Walk back and forth across the stage to make the audience follow you with their eyes.

◆ Act out the parts of the different people you talk about in your comedy.

Audio Effects And Vocal Characterizations

◆ Audio sound effects require a special talent but are great helps to painting a vivid picture.

◆ Vocal characterizations need not be full impressions, just distinct enough to suggest the presence of other people in your routines.

Concentration

◆ Concentration helps with your mental visualization and frees your imagination.

◆ When your concentration suffers, your show suffers.

Stage Presence

◆ It's not necessary to have rapid speech and an aggressive attitude to have a strong stage presence.

◆ Tattoo the words "commitment and conviction" in your brain for a strong stage presence.

◆ You must truly understand your point of view to have a strong stage presence.

Smooth Transitions

◆ Look for one-word connections or phrases that can help you get from one routine to another without it seeming disjointed (usually in your afterthought or tagline).

Structuring Your Funny (Writing Your Material)

Finding Your Pure Funny

To be able to write funny material for yourself, it's essential that you understand your own particular and natural "comedic essence." You want to write humor that captures the freshness of the humor that you do with friends when you're feeling relaxed and comfortable—it's at those moments when you are displaying your "pure funny." You have to learn how to observe and tap into that, because your "pure funny" is what you want to transport to the stage, and tapping into your "pure funny" or comedic essence is the quickest shortcut to writing funny material.

When I first started out as a comedian in 1971, my first impulse was to get a notebook and start to try to be deliberately funny and write some jokes. So I wrote down every half-baked zany thought that came into my head. I thought they were jokes, but the first club audiences I tried them on told me differently. I was devastated. For weeks I was totally lost, trying to figure out where I'd gone wrong. Finally I figured out that it started with the fact that my material wasn't me. I realized that I was trying to write material that went counter to the natural sense of humor that I had when I was with friends, and almost effortlessly making them laugh. It was what I thought a comedian's material should be, but it wasn't me. With my friends I wasn't trying to be funny—and I was. But when I started writing material and trying to be funny, I wasn't. So one night over ice tea and french fries (which I considered a treat given my poor student Raskolnikov-like existence), I threw out my notebook of laugh-free jokes and decided to start from scratch. I had to figure out how to recreate the sense of humor I had when I was relaxed with my friends.

Using The "Third Eye"

So I started using the "third eye" when I was with my friends in an attempt to understand what it was that made me funny with them. The third eye is a strange combination of detachment and heightened awareness that keeps you somewhat removed from a situation so that you can observe and record your thoughts and reactions. It's an instinctive way of remembering specific obscure details for recreation at a later date. For most artists, it operates on a subconscious level. Actors use it all the time. They remember and use gestures and attitudes from real moments in their lives to make their characters behave in a real fashion. For those of you who don't do this instinctively, you'll have to make a conscious decision to apply this technique. But it can be done quite easily. In the film All That Jazz, the Bob Fosse character (played by Roy Scheider) had an emotional argument with his lover (played by Ann Reinking). As he headed for the door, she said something particularly biting. Instead of answering back in kind, he stopped, reflected for a moment, and then went, "I'll have to use that." In the midst of this high-pitched excitement, the character's third eye was still at work, allowing him to make note of something that he could use in a creative endeavor.

When I was in law school and I'd get together with other students and spontaneously and inadvertently make them laugh, instead of just continuing the conversation, I would immediately stop and write in my ever-present notebook the line that made them laugh. And most importantly, I would put it in quotes so that I would know not to change or tinker with it in any way. Putting the line in quotes meant I had the laugh-producing line or lines in its pure form. Then later, when I had some time to myself, I would think about what it would take to make it funny for a bunch of strangers. The key was deciding if it depended on specific knowledge or had a universal context, which would then enable me to construct the appropriate setup. Through this process, I was able to zero in on my comedic essence and thus start generating funny material. By comparison, the previous jokes that I'd tried to write had been contrived.

If you are going to tap into your true pure funny you must make liberal use of the third-eye concept. It will give you insight and understanding of your true sense of humor and make its voyage from the safety of friends to the stage a relatively pain-free one. Surprise is a big element of comedy in that people are not expecting you to say what you say. When you spontaneously say or do something that makes your friends laugh, you have succeeded in catching them by surprise. Once you've created a setup for your already-proven laugh-getter, your punchline will catch the audience of strangers by surprise as well. Tapping into my pure funny relatively early allowed me to escape the months and sometimes years of bombing that many comedians go through.

Once you've used the third eye and tapped into your pure funny you are on the right track to writing the right material for yourself. Then all you have to do is start the process of what I call "structuring your funny."

Structuring Your Funny

In 1972 I was working in the men's department at a now-defunct clothing store in Century City in Los Angeles. One day a woman came in and bought a suit from me for her husband's birthday—with him to come in and be fitted the next day. When she handed me her credit card to complete the sale, it read Mrs. Bob Newhart, and the next day the comedian himself came in to be fitted. Seizing my chance as I measured his cuffs, I told him that I was an aspiring comedian and asked him the only burning question I could think of at the time: "How do you write your material?" He was very nice and understanding and told me that the most important thing was to outline the points that I wanted to talk about on the subjects that I chose. It was simple but extremely helpful advice, and having a good public-school education, I was able to immediately put outlining (something I learned in the fifth grade) into practice on those routines that I was creating out of my observations. Outlining a subject that you're interested in is a great way to deal with those routines that you want to consciously create, as opposed to those that spring forth spontaneously when with friends. It's essential for the aspiring comedian because it organizes your thoughts and gives them a spine to hang your humorous observations and embellishments on. When you outline and start to think about what you want to discuss, your subconscious will amaze you with all the things that it will reveal that you weren't aware that you'd noticed. This won't necessarily be a process that will have you laughing (though that's always a possibility). Rather, it's a serious thinking session where you jot down and order the odd or ironic things that have caught your attention. The first routine that I outlined concerned my observations about the old *Frankenstein*, *Dracula*, and *Wolfman* films. It was titled "Monsters In General" and the outline was as follows:

Monsters In General

A. Wolfman

  1. Won't mess with Wolfman 'cause he's faster than black people.

  2. When Wolfman catches you, he doesn't bullshit. You don't walk away with minor cuts and bruises.

B. Dracula

  1. All you need to deal with him is a cross, which you can get at any church or Klan meeting.

  2. If had a cross, I would torture him and steal his wallet.

C. Frankenstein

    1. So slow he can only catch you if you're with a girl, 'cause women in movies always fall down when chased by monsters.

    2. I would warn girl on date that if monsters chase us, I would be in the wind, so don't fall down.

Monsters In General was the first routine I outlined, and outlining it that way enabled me to think about what I wanted to say about what I had seen. And I never would've done it that way if I hadn't fitted Bob Newhart for a suit.

Choosing Topics

When you look across the spectrum of successful comedians and study their material, you will see a wide variety of subject matter that reflects their interests, and things that they've thought about a great deal. You'll also notice that much of the subject matter on first blush would seem to offer very little potential for humor, but that each comedian's point of view on the subject at hand has pointed out the many incongruities and ironies that make us laugh. Therefore, you should choose to talk about what you are truly interested in and concerned about because that will enable you to bring the full weight of your feelings and thoughts (a.k.a. your point of view) to the matter.

Dealing With Creative Block

The best weapon against creative block is to be tuned in to your point of view. Writing material is a journey not a destination. Don't try to force it. You may be dry of any funny observations or thoughts at the moment. Just accept that and get out into life, and live and observe. Your subconscious will be working even when you're not, because it knows your true point of view. Many times, I'd start a tour thinking that I didn't have any new ideas. But invariably things would start to come out of me on stage as the tour went on. These were fresh ideas that I didn't know I had, yet recognized like old friends because my subconscious had been making notes.

The most frightening time I had with creative block was in 1972 after I'd unexpectedly bombed at a Hoot Night at the Troubadour nightclub in Los Angeles. Not only did my new stuff written specifically for that evening bomb, but my previously successfully material bombed as well. My confidence in my ability to write humorous material was completely shattered, and I was feeling desperate. One night I ran into David Brenner at The Comedy Store in Los Angeles, and I asked him what to do. He said to just relax and not force it. He also told me to not think about being funny for a while. So that's what I did. I put the search for new material on the back burner and concentrated on just living my life. Soon I was getting off some good quips around my friends in conversation, making note of them, and was back on track for writing funny material.

Dealing with creative block effectively requires that you (1) Use the third eye to observe and record when you are exhibiting your natural comedic essence, and (2) Relax and trust the subconscious to do its job of absorbing images, thoughts, and ironies, and releasing its humorous conclusions into your conscious domain. That approach is best used when striving for a more spontaneous flow of creativity. The third, more-studied approach to attacking creative block is the one advocated by Jerry Seinfeld in his interview of just forcing yourself to sit down and wrestle with a premise. This way of dealing with creative block doesn't feel as good as the other way, but once you accept that it's going to feel like drudgery, you'll be amazed at how good some of the material is that you come up with. One of the greatest misconceptions about being an artist is that the creative process is always supposed to feel good. When the muse is in gear, it can be exhilarating. But more often than not, you'll have to consciously think your way through a comedy maze to a successful punchline. Believe it or not, this process can be just as satisfying because it feels so much more difficult. If you can continue fighting mentally on a "drudgery day," you'll go a long way toward making your next creative session flow that much easier. But if you give up with the intention of waiting for the muse, you may find that the next day is a drudgery-filled one was well. Grappling with a "drudgery day" will produce more usable material than you ever thought possible. The next day when you review material that might have come out in bone-breaking drips and drabs, you'll almost always be pleasantly surprised by how good some of it is. Not all of the material will be usable, but even the bad stuff can contain a germ of a good idea that can send you off in a promising direction.

Letting The Subconscious Mind Do Its Job

The subconscious mind is a little-considered but very important ingredient in the creative process. When you're out and about or reading newspapers or watching television, you don't need to conduct a frantic search for material. Instead, just go about your daily business, confident that your subconscious mind is absorbing impressions, attitudes, and details that will crystallize at the appropriate time. Just let the world flow over you with an alert mind, and you'll be amazed what comes out when you sit down to write your material. Ideas will pop out that you didn't even know you had.

Equipment For Creating Material

Always carry a microcassette recorder to record any thoughts and impressions that may occur to you. Don't try to keep the ideas in your head. Without fail, you'll forget them later. If you don't have a microcasette recorder, then carry a notebook. If you don't have either, then grab anything available to write on when you get an idea. When you get home, listen to the recorder, or read the notes

STRUCTURING YOUR FUNNY (WRITING YOUR MATERIAL)   29

you made, and transfer the ideas that you think are viable to a notebook, legal pad, or computer. Remember, don't trust your memory.

SUMMARY

To be able to generate and write good material you must:

◆ Use the "third eye" technique of observing yourself to tap into your "pure funny."

◆ Structure your funny by outlining the subjects you want to discuss.

◆ Choose topics that reflect your true interests and concerns.

◆ Deal with creative block by (1) understanding your point of view, (2) using the third eye, (3) relaxing and letting your subconscious mind work, or (4) accepting and grappling with "drudgery days."

◆ Carry a microcassette recorder or notebook with you at all times to record your ideas.

In Performance

Preparation For Your First Performance: Have A Plan

Let's say that you've decided to take the daunting step of going on stage at a club to see if you've got what it takes, comedically speaking. How do you prepare? First off, let me strongly suggest that you *do* prepare. Don't just go on stage without a thought, thinking you'll just wing it. You can do that if you want—just be prepared to be humbled like I was. My first time, I went up on stage with a vague sense of what I was going to talk about, confident that somehow, some way, I'd be funny. I took up half-baked (not even sautéed) ideas that, in the unforgiving glare of both the harsh spotlight and the equally harsh silence of the audience, were very clearly shown to be devoid of humor. In fact, totally worthless. I didn't know that the added stress of the situation would cause me to tighten up and not be able to think funny in the free-flowing way that I usually was with my friends and classmates. And this can all be traced to those first few crucial moments when the audience didn't laugh as I'd expected. Consequently, because I had thought I would just ad-lib, when the laughter didn't come, I had no idea where to go. I was totally lost. And unless you are extremely lucky or that rare genius, you'll be lost too.

Laughter is the lubricant that loosens the mind and creativity, and if it's not there, you'll lose confidence, which will affect your delivery, body language, timing, and everything else. After a serious performance post-mortem of a couple weeks, I concluded that the next time I went on stage, I would definitely have a plan that I would follow to the bitter end—win, lose, or draw. You must have a definite beginning and end to your maiden routine. You can always get away from it if things are going well and then ad-lib since you'll be doing it from a point of strength. But that's very hard to do from a point of weakness, which is where you'll be coming from if you go on stage without some sort of plan.

Preparation Of Material

You should start writing material at least two to three months (sooner than that if possible) before you plan to try your hand at stand-up on stage, because you want to accumulate a selection of routines to choose from. This is necessary because some of your routines are going to naturally be stronger than others. Even at this early date, you'll be forced to make choices, which is an underrated art in itself. You'll be preparing your first set list of routines—something you have to do your whole career when faced with different audiences and circumstances. Consequently, the ability to make good choices when faced with a variety of options is an absolute necessity and talent worth cultivating.

When I started to think about going back on stage after that first disaster, I wrote notes and routines in my notebook for months. I had no preconceived idea of how many routines to write, I just knew that I wanted a lot to choose from. When I finally sat down to decide what to use for my next set, I found the process of assessing the relative strength of the routines to be very stimulating and challenging. But more importantly, because each of these ideas and routines had been germinated from the "third-eye method" of spontaneous quips around friends during that period, I was choosing from a position of strength. After you've decided which routines you're going to use, start preparing the presentation by practicing and memorizing. I ran those first routines through my head every chance I got. It's amazing how diligent you can get when you think that telling jokes is the only way that you can escape living on the streets, asking for spare change. Soon, I knew those routines backwards, forwards, and sideways. Don't worry about losing your spontaneity and freshness, because the energy of the live audience will provide the spark to bring your routine alive again. Next, say the routines into a tape recorder for timing purposes. I found this to be a good idea for two other reasons: Number one, hearing some of the routines for the first time made me laugh and reinforced my gut feeling that they were comically viable. Secondly, hearing the routines also enabled me to see other comic tributaries and directions that were possible. Sometimes new lines were suggested to me that I hadn't thought of before. You must do this type of "mental weightlifting" in order to firm up your set. I'm not going to lie: It was very hard to make myself do this, but I did it because I just couldn't stand the idea of bombing again. The mere thought of that first time was—and still is—painful. But doing this hard work had dramatic benefits. I could perform free of unnecessary worry because I had confidence in my material, and my delivery of it. I was solid and ready to do battle.

An important note when putting together your first set: Always put what you consider to be your strongest material last. A strong ending can save a weak beginning, but not vice versa. It's a law of performing—the audience remembers how you end, not how you begin. If you start out bad or tentative, there's always the probability that you will relax more as the performance goes on, so by the time you get to your strongest material, your delivery will be at it's most relaxed and natural—allowing you to sell the routine in the right way and end your set with a good laugh.

Reasonable Goals For The First Time

Naturally, the goal that all aspiring comedians want to achieve when they first set foot on a stage is to have that magical night when everything they say makes the audience laugh. For a privileged few, that's just what happens. But for the majority of us mortals, even the most talented, closer to reality is getting a few nervous chuckles (if the audience is generous) or maybe not even that. That's why it's necessary to not only have a planned list of material, but to also have a well-thought-out set of reasonable goals that you want to achieve that have absolutely nothing to do with the amount of laughter that you do or don't receive. These goals should be concerned with developing one or more of the elements of comedy. Then, when you listen to the tape of your performance, you can judge how well these non-laughter-related goals were met. For example, you can set a goal that come hell or high water you'll make sure that your delivery is crisp, economical, and distinct. Or your goal can be to make sure that your concentration stays focused. With the mastery of each of your elements will come the laughter that you desire. If you realize that you are building a stand-up comedy act the same way that an athlete with big ambitions builds a tennis or golf game (slowly mastering each fundamental), you'll be able to live with the somewhat incremental nature of progress. More importantly, however, you'll be progressing to that day when you'll have the audience laughing at everything you say.

Nervousness

The best advice I can give you about being nervous is to not be afraid of it. Instead, use nervousness. I got this piece of advice from Johnny Carson right before he walked out on stage at *The Tonight Show* to deliver his opening monologue. I was a guest on the show that night, and I was more nervous than I usually was on club dates. I was backstage and saw him nervously fiddling with his shirt cuffs a couple minutes before the start of the show. "Don't tell me you still get nervous," I asked him incredulously. "Every night," he replied. When I told him how much I hated that nervous feeling, he told me not to be afraid of it but to use it. That one remark changed my outlook on being nervous, and it's something I never forgot. While I can—and prefer—to do a good show when I'm not feeling even a trace of pre-performance nerves, there are some performances (like television shows or showcases) where the appearance of nerves is inevitable. The thing that we all hate is that nervous feeling that everything that can go wrong will. But the onslaught of nerves is actually what prevents that from happening. Nervousness only signals that adrenaline is being pumped through your system, and adrenaline (as we all know) is what heightens our senses and speeds up our responses in times of danger. And it does the same thing when you're on stage. Nervousness alone will not make you fail, but if you're unprepared, it will. So do your preparation and embrace the nervousness knowing that your senses and mind are now as sharp as they'll ever be.

First-Time Pointers

1. Get to the club early. If possible go on the stage when the club is empty so that you can get a feel for the stage and soak in the environment.

2. Take your time when you step on the stage for your set. Don't rush to the microphone as many young comedians do. Set up your tape recorder, set the microphone height, and then begin. This subtly conveys to the audience an impression that you're confident, allows you to change the mood of the room, and helps prepare them for your own particular vibe or energy.

4. Let your energy build as you get into the flow of your set.

List Of Performance Goals

To help you with your performance goals, I'm going to show you the list of my personal performance goals that I've created and kept throughout the years. I came up with this list three years into my career after seeing Richard Pryor at The Comedy Store in Hollywood and marveling at his skills. Seeing him made me do an analysis on how to make my own performances stronger. I became particularly aware of the need to improve my audio and visual variety. While I knew that I didn't have the mimicking abilities that Pryor had, I still knew that I could improve in that area if I stayed cognizant of the need. To this day, I periodically consult this list and evaluate my progress. As you will see, my list of performance goals is all element related, with numbers one, five, and six being directly related to each other. The list is as follows:

1. To have a command of the stage and feel comfortable.
2. To add more power to my delivery.
3. To work routines more into a conversational flow without meandering.
4. To incorporate more visual and audio variety into my performance.
5. Keep my mind as free as possible in order to:
   a. relate to external stimuli
   b. allow for stream of consciousness
6. To add more abstraction and ad-libs to my performance.

The last goal was and is of particular interest to me because I knew that attaining it would add to the unpredictability and surprise that I wanted in my humor, as well as enable me to "write on stage" more and more as my confidence and command on stage grew.

Image/Persona Vs. The Real You

Don't be concerned too much about developing an image or persona when you're starting out. In fact, never consciously try to create one if you're trying to do humor based on your true point of view of life, society, the world, etcetera. Whatever you are will emerge naturally, though it will be in reality somewhat heightened when you're on stage. On stage, you are you plus fifteen percent. Richard Lewis, Richard Pryor, Woody Allen, Elayne Boosler, Bill Cosby, Garry Shandling, and many others have very distinct personas and comedic images that have emerged over the years. These personas are very close to the person that they are when they're not performing.

Trust Your Instincts

The reason you do all the necessary preparation is so that you can be free to trust your comedic instincts in the end. When you're on stage, you may get a feeling to stray from your plan, especially if you're doing well and getting some laughs. Go ahead and do it. See if your instincts are right or wrong. Say what's going through your mind. Surprise yourself and the audience. That's the only way you're going to learn what your comedy instincts on stage are—by either getting or not getting laughter with them. If it doesn't work, well, that's why you have a plan—so that you have something to go back to. In this same respect, don't be afraid if you make a mistake. Those are the times when you see if you have the comedy instincts to try and salvage some humor out of a slip. And frequently it can be done if you just acknowledge it. Audiences are actually ready to laugh, because they're relieved that you'll acknowledge the mistake—and thus on a more personal note their presence—as you would if you were with a friend.

The Proper Attitude

You must have the proper attitude or mindset when you start performing night after night through good times in your life and bad. One of the great difficulties is harnessing or disciplining the artistic nature in a way that doesn't stifle its creativity, but in fact enhances it. Many times, I didn't feel like doing a show but only did because I was working an engagement and had obligations to professionalism. Yet all those forced shows are what made me a stronger performer because they provided the stark reality of what being a professional comedian is. Doing it right—and good—when you don't feel like it. Former New York Yankee player Gil McDougal once said, "It's easy to have a good day when you're feeling good, and it's easy to have a horseshit day when you're feeling horseshit. The real trick is to have a good day when you're feeling horseshit." That's why having the proper attitude about performing is important. You must be mentally prepared each night to give people their money's worth—which basically means to clear your head and be prepared to concentrate for that time that you're on stage. After all, it's only an hour. The upside is that the more you concentrate the better job you'll do in creating laughs, which stimulates your creativity, resulting in more fun for both you and the audience.

Listen To The Audience

This is a very important thing for a comedian to do when performing. It's also something that a lot of comedians forget to do. Listen to their laugh and what type of laugh it is. There's the gentle chuckle, the ruminative chuckle, the laugh of recognition, the laugh of shock (both pleasant and otherwise), and the fully involved body laugh—which is the Moby Dick of laughs. One night at The Comedy Store in Los Angeles in the late 1970s I stood in the back of the room watching Richard Pryor perform a routine about sex. When he hit the punchline, "It's talking to you, daddy," I watched a whole room literally double over in uncontrollable laughter. In silhouette, I saw people spitting up drinks and falling out of their chairs. It was like a bomb had hit the room. I remember thinking at the time that I had just seen the "perfect guffaw." My goal became to try and get those kinds of laughs.

Note the "quality"—not just the quantity—of the laugh that you're getting. This is just as important—if not more—than just getting laughs. Cheap laughs are just that. Your jokes'll be treated just like Chinese food. In an hour, people'll be hungry for another comedian. In addition to listening to the audience's laugh, you want to listen to their silence. Is it bored or interested silence? The silence is quieter and filled with energy when they're interested. You can hear a pin drop. When they're bored, you can always hear it. Thirdly, listen to yourself periodically as well so that you can hear your delivery. Listening to the audience enables you to better build a genuine rapport in the same way that listening to an individual allows you to better interact with them. It allows you to better gauge where you stand with them and what type of material to use.

Hecklers

The following is an excerpt from a journal I kept in 1989 for an article on comedy for *Playboy*. It concerns handling a heckler during a show in Houston.

Monday, October 24—Houston

I did a one-hour-and-50-minute show—the longest set I've done in ages. Plus, I had two hecklers. My first tactic with a heckler is to ignore him. Thank goodness, most hecklers say stupid things, and you can usually hang them in a short time if you need to. It took ten minutes before my first heckler could be embarrassed into silence. I was boiling inside—if a heckler takes up too much of your time, it's difficult to get back to your prepared material. I won the audience back, and I was cruising when the second heckler hit—an hour and forty minutes into the show. I said, "Look man, I dealt with one cat, I don't need this. Y'all take it easy," and I started to walk off the stage. The rest of the audience said, "No, no, come on back," and intimidated the heckler. In fact, the first heckler offered to shut him up for me.

Afterward, a couple of people said, "Man, you handled those hecklers so well. You were so relaxed." When I told them how infuriated I was inside, they seemed surprised. "You're very lucky. Your anger doesn't show," one of them said.

That excerpt relates an experience that taught me two things. First, that the bulk of an audience comes to see the comedian, not the heckler. If you're entertaining them and you give them a choice, they're gonna choose you. Secondly, I learned that as angry as I was in my mind, which was reflected (to me at least) in the cutting nature of my remarks to the heckler, to the audience I didn't appear unduly angry.

Handling hecklers is directly related to how well you listen to the audience because that's what's going to help you deal with them. Over the years I've learned that most hecklers are poor comedians, and that the things they yell out are usually stupid and easily dissected. Dealing with a drunk heckler can be like shooting fish in a barrel. Their usually inane remarks will give your wit an easy target. Listen real close to what they say, and it will suggest its own obvious quick response. Sometimes, I just repeat slowly the stupid thing they've just said. Remember, the audience is on your side if they've been enjoying the show, so it doesn't have to be a killer response, just appropriate. After all, the reason you're on the stage is supposedly because you have the quicker wit, and nine times out of ten you will.

Sometimes a heckler can be good for your show, particularly if you're at a point where you don't have any new material and you're a little bored with your act. Dealing with a heckler can be a chance for you to play around and see how your mind handles fresh stimuli.

Bombing And How To Deal With It

Bombing. Dreaded, unavoidable, necessary. For a comedian, bombing at one time or another is an inevitable reality. Like a person who applies to be a fireman, you know that eventually you're going to have to walk into a burning building. That's the occupational hazard. Especially at the beginning. There isn't a comedian I've interviewed for this book who didn't have some period of bombing when they started out. But they all persevered and learned from those times. In fact, bombing teaches you how badly you want to become a comedian. Because unless it's a burning desire, you'll quit when the consistent bombing becomes too much to take. It's what separates the men from the boys, the women from the girls, the dogs from the cats, the mice from the rats. What you have to be able to do is to try and figure out why you bombed, which is easier after you've been doing it a while with some success. When you're starting out, it's very important to tape your shows and listen to them—no matter how terrible they are. You'll be able to hear more objectively where your delivery was ineffective, or where your timing and pauses were wrong, or where you were rushing, or how confusing your thinking or setup was. All the little things that are necessary for a good stand-up comedy performance can be scrutinized, and corrected for the next time. In the initial stages of your development, your ability to use the elements of comedy will be understandably shaky since that's when you'll be your most nervous. But as you get more relaxed on stage, your use of those elements will grow. The biggest area to focus on, however, will be whether you're being true to your point of view and explaining it clearly to the audience.

The best advice I can give to anyone who is bombing is to do your performance evaluations and then get back on stage. Just like in football or baseball, you have to get up off the ground and keep coming back. That's the only way you'll develop into a good comedian. As my clarinet teacher used to say, "Nobody's born great. You can't get good if you can't take the punishment."

Evaluating A Performance

It's important that you listen to a tape and grade or evaluate each of your performances in a serious manner, so that you can give yourself an idea of where you're strong and where you need to improve. For the first two years, I graded every performance with a letter grade. And I wasn't easy on myself either. I tried to be as objective as I could. The following are two evaluations from those early days.

Performance Evaluations

1. Club: Troubadour 10/09/72 Grade: C

    A. Stage Presence - Pretty good. Kept composure though didn't do well.

    B. Concentration - All right but slipped a few times. Ad-libbed okay.

    C. Delivery - Spoke much too fast and made it difficult for audience to understand.

    D. Material - On the whole did not go over well at all.

        1 Don't think Troubadour audience liked overt sexual stuff.

        2. However, did material as planned (didn't botch it).

    E. Hints (Lessons Learned)

        1. Do more topical material at Troubadour

        2. Don't open with controversial stuff

        3. Work more on "Militant Meeting" material

        4. Do more satirical material

2. Club: Comedy Store 11/11/72 Grade: B

    A. Stage Presence - Good, but could be more relaxed.

    B. Concentration - Needs improvement. Mind wandered.

    C. Material - Well received

D. Timing - Good

E. Hints (Lessons Learned)

1. Work on "Coach Show" routine

2. Drop "Anti-Drug Commercial" bit

3. Don't talk as fast

4. Prepare better opening

SUMMARY

Preparation for your first time on stage should be thorough and well planned. In order to have a good plan, you should do the following:

◆ Start to write material at least two to three months before you go on stage. This material should be routines that you've developed using the third-eye method. Don't go on stage for the first time thinking you'll just ad-lib your way through. The pressure is too great for a novice.

◆ Memorize your routines until you know them backwards and forwards.

◆ Talk your routine into a tape recorder to get an idea of how long it runs.

◆ Put your best routine at the end so that you can finish strong. A good finish can make up for a bad beginning, but not vice versa.

Doing Television Talk Shows

Like a fairy tale, there once was a time when doing one great spot on a late-night talk show like *The Tonight Show* or *David Letterman* could be an almost-guaranteed launching pad to immediate success and full houses at comedy clubs. Sadly, that day is no more. Due to the saturation of comedy-club shows and specials filled with indistinguishable comedians on the many cable networks over the years it's gotten much more difficult to make that type of galvanizing impression in the nation's consciousness in one swoop like a Roseanne, a Flip Wilson, a Freddie Prinze, and generate what people in the industry call "heat." To build a national following with one spot is indeed a thing of the past. However, these shows are still very valuable because people in the industry still monitor talk shows for new talent. So it's still very important from a career standpoint to do them whenever possible. It's just gonna take you a series of successful spots to build up your national profile.

I must confess that it took me a while to learn how to do spots up to my standards on the late-night talk shows—mainly because of my somewhat free-form style. It was very hard for me to adapt to talk shows' five- to six-minute spots after doing hour long nightclub shows, and also because of my nervousness. I wasn't able to showcase myself to my satisfaction on television until I did one very important thing: I started treating television as though it were just another night at a club. I stopped ruminating continuously over my television set and thinking about its potential significance. This started with my last few shots with Johnny Carson when I realized why my spots hadn't seemed as funny to me as my club sets. I realized that the extra thought and preparation actually worked against me. Once I adopted this new attitude, I started doing television spots that I was happy with. But let me stress that this was just my approach. I know many successful comedians who still prepare their television spots very diligently and exhaustively. Larry Miller (an outstanding comedian and actor) used to do as many as three different spots a night for weeks, running his *Tonight Show* set when preparing for a spot.

Television Vs. Nightclub Audiences

Obviously, the most difficult thing about doing a spot on television versus the normal nightclub set is the fact that you have a very short time to score. Five minutes to be exact on *The Tonight Show*. You have to get them fast on TV, whereas in a club you have some time to work into your act and rhythm. But the good thing is that you don't have to warm the audience up because TV studio audiences are already warmed up and excited. Thus, you have an audience that's already very receptive to you, whether the viewers at home are or not. But it's the studio audience that's important because they're the ones you have to hear laugh. Give no thought whatsoever to the people watching television because you can't hear them. Play to the studio audience only. If they're laughing, the people at home are laughing. A lot of times, managers, agents, and people who know you will always stress how many millions of people will be seeing you. Ignore that. Don't even think about it (unless of course that type of information energizes you and makes you perform better). Some people like to put extra pressure on themselves to do well by always concentrating on the significance of an event. It doesn't do anything for me. I work better in pressure-filled situations when I take the attitude that it's just another day or club, though I do have a little more adrenaline pumping. If you're the same way, it's best that you recognize it and prepare yourself accordingly. Different strokes for different folks. But I advise treating the studio audience like a nightclub audience because that's the reason you're doing television—to get them to come see you in a nightclub.

With respect toward material, obviously you're going to be doing your best current stuff on your television spot. But you may have to change the density of the material, depending on the type of comedy you do. If you do one-liners, very little change will be necessary. You'll just have to time your lines. But if you do stories, or material with a lot of tags, or afterthought lines, you'll probably have to cut those out. In other words, you'll have to strip-mine your material and "lean" it up to fit the time constraints. At least, that's what I found I've had to do to get my set ready for television. Afterthought or tag lines after a good punchline add to your act in a club, but take away on television, due to a very interesting audience phenomena: I don't know how or why it got started, but television studio audiences applaud funny lines much more frequently than nightclub audiences, and thus make you stop and wait to deliver your "tag" lines, which can then seem anti-climatic and momentum-losing. Plus, that extra applause, nice as it may be, eats into your time out there, and could cause you to rush later, even better routines as you built to your close. So be prepared to cut your little extra lines that come after a big punchline and move on to the next joke or routine to give your set more punch and crispness. You can keep them in your set, but if the audience applauds your big line, don't do your tag when it dies down, just move on.

One of the most important things to keep in mind when you're doing television is that you can't run over. These shows are very tightly structured, particularly with respect to commercial breaks. But you'll have help keeping this together because the stage manager will give you a signal. He or she'll be standing in front of you by a camera and will either hold up a sign or a hand signal letting you know to wrap it up. I usually ask them to give me a one-minute signal. You can ask them before the show to give you whatever time signal you want. They're very happy to help you.

Get There Early

Just like when you first work a club, I advise people doing their first shot on any show to get there early before the audience is brought in, walk out on the studio floor, and familiarize yourself with the mark where you'll be standing, where the cameras will be (though you really shouldn't worry about them), and get the feel of the room. Look around, walk around, soak it in until you feel comfortable so that you don't just walk out cold into a brand-new performing environment under pressure. This is very helpful to minimize your nervousness.

Doing Panel

Being funny—sitting down. That's what doing panel is for a comedian. Doing panel well is actually more important than doing a good stand-up spot because it's when the audience observes you in a more "conversational" mode and decides if they like your personality—which is one of the real keys to popularity. And you have to prepare that spot (usually two minutes) just as you do your stand-up spot. The talent coordinator or segment producer prepares a series of jokes or subjects, and will ask you what kind of questions the host can ask. So when you decide on what kind of jokes you plan to do for your panel segment, give a lot of thought to the type of questions that can get you easily into the subjects. If you have a conversational-like delivery already, it won't be hard for you to shine. You'll find as you look through your routines that some of your material will actually be better suited to a panel presentation than a stand-up one, particularly if you have a few non-sequitur attitudinal one-liners that just need a question asked. This way you can get them exposed through your panel segment.

Rather than play to the audience, I find that it's better to play to the host as though in a real conversation and let the audience listen in—which they are. The camera will be on your face—don't worry about that. If it's funny, the audience will laugh. If they don't but the host does, even better. Because just like anybody else, they'll have the people on their show who amuse and entertain them. (For more about doing late-night television shows and panel, see the Richard Lewis interview).

SUMMARY

◆ Treat the studio audience like a nightclub audience. Relate to them exclusively.

◆ Be prepared to lose tag or afterthought lines from your routine for television, because television studio audiences applaud clever lines and cut into your time.

◆ Get to the studio early so that you can familiarize yourself with its environment and get the feel of the room.

◆ Look through your routines and think of questions that can be asked to get you into them for your panel segment. Make these routines as conversational as possible.

Part II

COMIC INSIGHTS
(Conversations With Comedians On The Art Of Stand-Up)

*If people come away relating to me as a
person, rather than just enjoying my jokes.
If they come away wanting to hear me
again no matter what I might talk about.
Then I'm succeeding.*
—Woody Allen

LOUIE ANDERSON
"It's Honesty, Don't You Think?"

In 1987, I did a movie titled *The Wrong Guys* in Jackson Hole, Wyoming, with fellow comedians Louie Anderson, Richard Belzer, Tim Thomerson, and Richard Lewis. Before I was signed to do the movie I had never met Louie or seen his act. Ironically, just before departing for Wyoming, I inadvertently met Louie at the American Comedy Awards in Los Angeles. Coincidentally, Louie's Showtime special was showing that month, and I had the opportunity to watch it. I was struck by the way he took his time setting up his routines, the subtle way he used his eyes in the close-ups, and how space or silence was an entity within itself in Louie's act. It was a revelation seeing him work in that leisurely yet crisp fashion. He is a master of timing and space. Unlike the many comedians who speak fast and aggressively to the audience, Louie takes his time and leisurely draws a vivid picture. Pauses and subtle manipulations of his face and body contribute to the total humorous effect that he is trying to create. He is a storyteller.

When we arrived in Wyoming to film, Louie and I were asked to share a condominium for the first two weeks of filming due to a snafu with our housing arrangements. We got along great, and Louie proved to be very resourceful about getting food for us at night. One evening we returned to a foodless condo, and Louie wanted to have a pizza. I mentioned that there were no pizza shops nearby and we didn't have a car. Louie looked at me incredulously and said,

"Look at me. Trust me, I know how to get food." Thirty minutes later a guy just showed up at the door, and we had a pizza. At that time, Louie weighed 350, down from a high of 450. When I told him that he didn't look 350, he said, "Oh yeah? You'd think it if I laid on you." Another incident that stands out is the time that Louie was leaving to go see the movie, *Adventures in Babysitting*. When I asked him why he wanted to see that particular film, he said, "Well, it's the type of movie that I want to write about . . . kids and stuff. I want everybody to see my movie. You see, I had a really horrible family life, and if I can bring a family together for an hour and a half, that's a big thing for me." He later had a TV cartoon called *The Louie Show*. When I ran into him, Louie said he was glad to be doing it because, "I can recreate my family."

I had a very pleasant two weeks rooming with Louie. In fact I would've liked to room together the whole shoot, but when they notified us that his condo was ready, Louie moved out. He told me, "Nothing personal, but I had eleven kids in my family. I have to live alone." Nevertheless, during our time together we had some lengthy talks about stand-up comedy, the road, filmmaking, and his philosophic approach to performing stand-up. This interview was conducted in 1987.

LOUIE ANDERSON

Louie, let's talk a little bit about the road.

I try not to do the road anymore.

You don't like it?

No.

What is it you don't like?

I especially don't like flying and I don't like . . . you know, one town to the other. It's very hard on people.

It's lonely, isn't it?

Yeah, it is. And it's just no fun. The performing part—the one hour that you perform—is fun, but then you've got twenty-three hours to think about the fact that you're not home.

And walk through malls?

Yeah. I have over three thousand candles from buying stuff at malls.

How do you handle those hours on the road without getting into bad habits?

I used to go to antique shops and see some historical stuff. You know, try to find a good restaurant. But it gets old. When I toured with Roseanne, it was a little easier because there was someone else you could talk to, and we had a lot of fun.

Your act is centered a lot around your father. Has this allowed you to work out some of the problems you had?

Yeah, I think a lot of my act is working out the problems I've had with my family, my father in particular. And I think that it really makes a difference. And I think it's healthy and helpful.

Is it cathartic for you?

Yeah, I would say. I would say less now than it was because I've worked it out.

Can comedy come out of joy or must it always come out of some type of sadness or pain?

I haven't been able to figure that out. I think that comedy just comes out of you. And I think whatever kind of person you are, that's the kind of comedy that comes out. I think that half of how a joke is formed, or how comedy is formed, is the right mixture of a lot of different things in that individual. It's like ingredients go into you, like maybe a rough childhood, an oversensitive heart, an intelligent mind, and then maybe a defiance and rebellion. And I think all those things go in the right combination, and then they come out as a joke or as a monologue.

How do you feel about stardom, Louie? How do you handle it?

Well, popularity is how I like to look at it more than anything else, because stardom is such an ambiguous thing, and it doesn't make any sense to anybody anyway. What's important for me is to continue to be creative, to continue to deal with the public like I do deal with them, and also to grow creatively because, if you're not growing, then the stardom doesn't mean anything. So, I keep challenging myself.

Is it hard for you to challenge yourself?

No. Actually, I feel bad when I'm not working and challenging myself. That's what it's all about. It's like a gift. As soon as you stop servicing the gift, you lose it.

How does one service the gift of creativity?

By always taking a bigger chance. No matter if you fail or not.

So, you never have the tendency to play it safe? You're working new material every show?

Yeah, I try to work on new material every day.

What are your writing habits like when you work on your act?

I never write anything down. It's all in my head.

You never write anything down?

Never.

Did you have any influences when you were starting out?

Uh-huh. Jonathan Winters influenced me a lot, Richard Pryor with his performance skills.

Who's the best stand-up you've seen so far in your time?

As a performer, Richard Pryor. As a writer and innovator, it would have to be Lenny Bruce. He is the man who made everything possible. Bill Cosby is a genius in giving a role model for black people and never commenting on it. That is a very clever thing.

How do you deal with hecklers?

Very quickly.

Have you had any lingering hecklers who've disrupted the show?

I've had hecklers who have ruined shows, but I leave. See, when I go into a club, I find out who's the doorman, and I sit down with him, and I ask him if there's anything that he needs from me. And then he usually asks if there's anything I need from him. And I'll say the one thing I need is as soon as somebody heckles me, I want you on him. I will respond once to the person in a friendly, nice way. If he says it again, I'll do my second line, and if he does it again, you should be tapping on his shoulder, saying, "I'm sure you're having a lot of fun, but really, save your comments for yourself because it ruins the show for everybody else." And then I say if he does it a fourth time, then you should be removing him. Mostly you only have to tell people one time when they're heckling, but when they're drunk, then forget it.

You say that Richard Pryor influenced you. It seems that among comedians, the consensus is that Richard is the best. Why is that?

He did it all. He was more than a comedian.

What was he?

I don't know, but he had a special extra ingredient. Richard was the best at surgically opening himself up on stage . . . like his whole guts and everything, and laying it out on display. I think he was best at displaying his insides, and that's why you loved him so much because he'd go up there and you'd go, This guy is hiding absolutely nothing from me, and he's being completely honest, but yet he's funny and he's right and he's making me think but he's not making me feel guilty about what I am.

Who are some of your other favorite comedians?

Jonathan Winters, Jackie Gleason. Bob Hope, great timing. But the guy who influenced me more timing-wise was Jack Benny. He had the best timing of all. Nobody had better timing than Jack Benny. At least anybody I could find. I like Carson, too. I think Carson had great timing.

Let's talk about timing for a second. The way I think about timing is use of space. Silence. That seems to be something that a lot of comedians don't seem to use well.

They don't know how. The secret behind timing is to hold whatever you're going to say until you absolutely have to say it.

How do you adjust your timing to network TV, say like a talk show where the audience is accustomed to the comedian going fast in that six-minute slot?

I just say, do it my way. I'll do a take for four, five, six seconds (which is unheard of), but the sooner you do it, the sooner they get into your rhythm.

It seems to me that television studio audiences respond differently to a clever line than nightclub audiences in that they burst into applause, whereas in a nightclub the audience just laughs. The applause throws my timing off a little bit because I'm waiting for the laugh.

For me, what works when they do that is I completely ignore it, and wait until it's done. Like, they never gave it to me. If I acknowledge it, I break my concentration, and if I break my concentration, I break my confidence, and if I break my confidence, I'm no longer in charge. But one thing I've learned on television is that you can wait a little longer and you won't lose 'em. If you rush it, you'll fuck it up.

I watched your special before we went to Wyoming, and I was really amazed at how subtle you were. You do a lot of things with your eyes. It was a very subtle presentation, and it gave me faith that that type of comedy could still be done in this day and age.

I like to believe that the audience is smart, and I refuse to hit people over the head with my lines.

Do you tape your live performances?

I used to, but now I videotape on stage, which teaches me even more. I bought a little 8-millimeter Sony video camera. And it takes great pictures. And then I can sit back and look and see what I'm doing wrong.

That's great. I've always just done my analysis of my performance from an internal source.

I used to have a lot of bad habits on stage that I corrected.

For example?

I would always play to one side. Instinctively, I would just play to that right side. And I changed that. I like to have a mike in my hand, but I quit doing that to learn about television, and I also worked on my movement. I found out that a lot of movement was better than a lot of words. A lot of expressions would get me a lot more mileage than any word, 'cause if I just give the expression, then you have to make up the word and your word will be stronger than mine ever could be.

A concept that I think successful comedians have, is the ability to find the essence of what is funny about them. And a lot of comedians can't find that.

Yeah, it always surprises me how dumb some comics are about certain things. I don't mean it in a derogatory way, I just mean that I've said to people, "I think if you did it this way, it would work better for you." And they're always amazed that they didn't know it.

What I'm talking about is more like you'll be with a comedian and they're funny off stage when you talk to them, but when they go on stage, they seem to do humor that is totally different from them as a person. It seems to me that they haven't realized what their natural funniness is. I think that the best comedians take their natural funniness, sense of humor, or whatever up on stage.

You're right. It's honesty, don't you think? I think all great comics have been able to do one thing that other comics haven't.

Which is?

They've been able to connect their heart to their head. If you can connect your heart to your head, then you can really get the most out of the whole situation.

Can you do that?

Yeah, I do it all the time.

I'm going to throw some names out and I want you to characterize their comedy. Richard Lewis.

His comedy is very, very intellectual, because of the images and the references.

That makes it difficult for a mass audience to grab on, wouldn't you say?

Sometimes. Especially the masses in this country. I think other countries are more intellectual.

Richard Belzer.

Political. Social elements. A lot of them.

Myself.

Warm, sweet, and with a message.

That's interesting. Jay Leno?

Mechanic. Boom-boom-boom. Just has an incredible amount of material.

How about the content?

Good. Discerning.

Robin Williams?

Complete recall. Remembers every single thing he's ever heard.

Roseanne.

A great comedian. Not just a woman doing comedy, but with a tremendous delivery, attitude, and a message to a lot of people out there—especially women. But most of all, funny.

A lot of women don't make men laugh. Why is that?

Because it's not their position or role in society. It's a man's world, stand-up comedy, but if you're funny, you can get into it whether you're a woman or not.

RICHARD BELTZER

"We're Riders On The Storm"

If Rasputin had been a comedian, he would've looked like Richard Belzer or The Belz as he's known. A legend in the New York comedy-club scene of the seventies and eighties, he's one of the few comedians to be featured on the cover of *Rolling Stone*. Then known for his funny, bristling anger, volatility, and self-destructive tendencies, Richard got a good grip on himself after a successful bout with cancer. Over the years his persona has evolved from the bitter and profane Belz into the sardonic, world-weary Munch on the NBC police drama *Homicide: Life on the Streets* (and later *Law & Order: Special Victims Unit*), where he has been able to put his distinctively acerbic delivery to optimal effect in the service of great dialogue. What a marriage. The Belzer that I came to know when we worked on the film *The Wrong Guys* in 1987 is very much like the character John Munch. A serious and voracious reader, he is well-informed on many subjects. Each morning in the van on the way to the set, he would hold forth on a wide-ranging number of subjects. One day I hung out with Richard in town as he excitedly shopped for some flowers for his wife, actress Harlee McBride (Dr. Dyer on *Homicide*) who was coming to Wyoming for a visit. At a bookstore, he purchased a book by Carl Jung for light reading during the shooting, which I ribbed him about. He takes his comedy very seriously as well, as I discovered the night I conducted this interview in 1987.

RICHARD BELZER

How long have you been doing stand-up?

Since '71. Yeah, I'm an old motherfucker.

Where'd you start?

I started in New York, at Catch A Rising Star and Kenny's Castaway.

Did you have influences when you started?

I was always into comedy. Even as a little kid, I was a student of comedy. I loved comedians and studied them.

Just instinctively?

Yeah, as long as I can remember.

Who first stood out to you when you were a kid?

Jack Benny, Groucho Marx, Laurel & Hardy, W.C. Fields, and then I remember Lenny Bruce when I first heard him in the fifties.

I had never heard of him until the day he died. Comedy seems to be fueled by a lot of anger. Why is that?

I think a lot of people in comedy are sitting on a lot of anger, and comedy is a way, obviously, to relieve that.

Do you feel it really relieves it?

Yeah, I do.

How so?

If I wasn't able to consistently perform on a consistent basis, then whatever happens when I perform, however that serves my psychological make-up, my spiritual make-up, however it serves that—if I don't have that outlet, then I would be different somehow. I don't know how. I don't know what I would do. It's literally unimaginable to me.

Is that the primary reward that you get from stand-up?

That's not the only thing. The thing I resent is the pervasive view of comedians that they must be either really depressed or really angry because they are in this. I don't like the characterization we get as the sad clown, or the guy who's always on. I bridle at that. It makes it pathological. And even though there are a lot of people in comedy who are depressed and angry, it still shouldn't dilute the art form itself. Which is, as you know, one of the few art forms indigenous to this country: jazz, abstract painting, and stand-up comedy.

Is suffering necessary for art?

From my own personal experience, I think that it's kind of an emotional elitism for artists to claim that situations like death, divorce, and all these things are incorporated in their art. I think that trivializes the emotion itself.

And yet you find young artists emulating the behavior of the "tragic artist" of all stripes.

Totally missing the point. The tragedy that visits most great artists was not consciously sought out by them, but introduced into their lives. Creativity's a blessing and a curse. If you don't tend to it, it can do other things to you. That's why we feel so good when we're being creative—because we're doing the right thing.

Are you disciplined?

No, I'm the laziest. I have to be forced to do a job. I have to get a job to do it.

You're deadline-oriented?

Yeah.

Do you look forward to performing each night?

No. Sometimes I hate it and I don't want to do it and I get depressed and I want to run away. Sometimes I feel real relaxed, and it's always different. Sometimes I don't know if I'm up to the task.

It is a task, isn't it?

Oh yeah, man. The only people who realize what it takes to do it are those who do it. There's no way to verbalize what we do, that feeling of putting your soul on the line. We're riders on the storm.

Have your goals in comedy changed over the years?

The older I get, the less I set goals, because the older you get, the more you realize how unpredictable life is, how brutal life is, and how unprepared we are—no matter how much we know. Obviously I make plans and have goals, but nothing surprises me anymore. That's why we have to be like warriors and always be ready for death any second.

That sounds like those Japanese Bushido warriors. Do you read much Eastern philosophy?

I've read tons of it. Mostly yoga philosophies. I was into yoga and a vegetarian for four years. Not for health reasons but for philosophical reasons. And then I passed out of that stage.

I used to read some Zen as a concept—a way to approach life. Also some Stoicism, the I Ching and Confucius. I never had a big ego, but I knew that I needed to compete with people with big egos, so I thought the Oriental approach seemed to be the most sensible approach to being able to compete without as much ego involved.

I think that Oriental thought invests more dignity in the individual than Western religions. Western religions tend to depict humanity as dirty and sinful. I love the idea of Christ, but as Nietzche said, the only true Christian was Jesus. Everybody else is scamming.

Are you as angry as you were ten years ago about life and society?

I think I have more ways of being taken seriously by the culture, so that anger has dissipated some. I don't know if I'm less angry, or if it's that now I have more ways of saying what I have to say, so that the anger is expressed. I don't think that diminishes the anger, but I think it diminishes the tension over not being able to release it. Now I have several forums that I didn't have years ago.

Is it important to you to be taken seriously?

I want to affect other people's lives in a positive way. And if I can take current events and illuminate them and make people think about it in a different way and laugh at it and be educated, then that's really where it's at.

So, ultimately there's an altruism in your humor?

It's not by design. I don't think I have this great moral inside track, but I guess that's what makes me feel the best, so it just happens to be. There's a great power to comedy. The idea of making a bunch of strangers laugh and share the same thing at the same moment is a very profound metaphysical and physical force. To be able to do that can be taken for granted or it can be thought of as a responsibility. Let's put it this way—it's my religion.

ELAYNE BOOSLER
"I Covet The Art Of It"

I've known Elayne Boosler for a number of years, and I've always had tremendous respect for her talent and tenacity. She is the epitome of an "independent individual." I had the pleasure of working with Elayne on two occasions in the early eighties. On one occasion we performed a one-nighter at a high-school prom in Philadelphia at 3:00 a.m. We came into Philadelphia from different parts of the country and only had time to talk a little bit. The second time we performed together was a two-day college tour in Washington State. We flew small commuter airlines to get to a couple of hard-to-reach schools, and also rode in a car together for significant distances. We got to know each other much better as we talked about a great many things. During this two-day period, the conversation got around to the way we were doing our personal-appearance business. Elayne surprised me when she revealed that she did not have a manager or an agent by choice, and that she did all the negotiations with club owners herself. It is rare when an artist can be both an artist and a business person with equal proficiency, and Elayne is one of the best at this difficult task, and is resolute in her determination not to be denied what she rightly feels she has earned. She was adamant with club owners that she would not accept less money than her male counterparts and would turn down work indefinitely if she had to.

Though she is not easily intimidated, she does not hide behind bravado, and in our conversations her vulnerability was readily apparent. Elayne gives credence to the saying, "Courage is fear that has said its prayers." Her thoughts and strategies about negotiating made quite an impression on me, and gave me insights into how to take a firmer hand on my own career.

Since the time we worked together, Elayne has forged a strong national comedic identity through continual creativity, hard work, and savvy business dealings. Her thoughts and strategies about negotiating made quite an impression on me, and I felt that she would be an invaluable speaker to show my students that it is possible for an artist to take a cool, practical approach toward the managing their own career without diminishing their creative abilities and output. This question and answer was conducted in my class during the summer of 1992.

ELAYNE BOOSLER

What motivated you to take total control of your career? No manager or agent, doing all your negotiating, and so forth?

That was a necessity. I had no one to help. I still do it. I don't have an agent or a manager. I do everything. I have a company, and I have people who work, but they don't negotiate, and they don't choose where to go. They execute the contract, they follow up, and they get the deposits. I get the work, and I create the opportunities and force the projects. If there's no job, you have to give yourself a job. I think people assume that when you reach a certain level of expertise, the work'll all come to them. For some lucky people that does happen. It happened to Robin Williams and Freddie Prinze, but for most people it doesn't happen like that. They do a first great *Tonight Show* or HBO *One Night Stand*, and they think that's it, man, the doors open up and the gold falls through. I've been doing this since 1973, and I know what that initial kind of rush is, and it's wonderful, and you try to build on it as much as you can. But if you're not Robin Williams, who is really the only one I can think of who's alive who was able to keep going all the way, it becomes a fight. Even Billy Crystal had a big rush and then fell back for about eight years. The point is, it's a relay, not a quick sprint. It's what happens to you after that first rush. It's the ability to keep going, and what sustains you is the reason you're in it. If you're in it for that first quick thing because you want to use comedy as a stepping stone to get a show, then great, get one thing and try to get a show. But if you're in it to be a comedian, which most people aren't these days, then your thing is to be on the road trying to develop five new jokes and being happy that they worked. The thing is to be happy where you are. I've been on the road nineteen years. I like where I am. I take a lot of pleasure in the work.

What is the pleasure of the work to you?

I covet the art of it. I really love the creation of stand-up. I write scripts, I do other things, but there's nothing like this for me. I've written four Showtime one-hour concerts, and I'm excited by the fact that after nineteen years I can write a whole new hour that's current, topical, and works. The reason to keep writing is to find out what you're thinking now.

Does this mean that you must continually change subjects?

Not necessarily. If you wrote about dating in your last special, you can still write about dating because it's two years later, and you can figure out what dating is to you now. You start over as if you've never written about it before. You have to be interested in what you're thinking, plus you must be non-introspective about anything else. When I'm being interviewed on tour, they ask me all these questions, and I don't have the answers.

When you had to develop a new hour for a special, what did you do?

I booked a solid tour. I worked every single night. I booked concerts all over for the weekend and for the weekdays. I'd find a club halfway between the two points that wouldn't interfere in ticket business for the concerts, and I'd work there. I don't think I had a night off in eight months. I just kept building and taping. I don't write, I just go on.

So you do all your writing on stage, and then listen to the tape?

Yes, except I hardly listen to the tape. I remember where I should listen on the tape. Sometimes I do a line on stage that comes out perfect, and I can't get it again, so I listen to the tape to hear how I said it originally.

Did you start out writing on stage?

Always. I'd read the paper and I'd get riled up, and then I'd go on stage.

Do you ruminate over what you've read that day and develop your material in your mind?

The paper doesn't change every day. The abortion fight's going on, the economy's been going on. This is all four to eight years old already. So it just festers. Someone once said to me, "I've figured you out. You either want to be outrageous or outraged." I can live with that. I don't enjoy the jokes that are just jokes for me as much as the jokes that have a little political punch on the end.

Do you tailor any material to the particular city that you're in?

Whatever city I'm in, I read their paper because I think it's just great if you can go up and bounce off ten or twenty minutes of local news because you're an outsider coming in and looking at them. They're kind of stuck in there discussing it with each other and a whole new breeze comes in and they're very entertained by how you see it.

So you're basically doing what Mort Sahl does? Coming so much out of the daily news?

Yeah, though I think he's on a higher level of political education than I am. I basically deal with stuff that really bothers me.

How do you keep track of your material since you don't write anything down?

If I get kicked in the head by a horse I'm dead. There's no files.

When you're writing on stage and something bombs, do you fall back on old material?

Thank God, that's never happened to me. When I'm putting together a special, sometimes I'll announce it in the paper. That way they'll know some stuff'll be rough. But the thing is that at this stage, I don't end each sentence and wait for a laugh. I don't even need anybody to be there really. My style is so conversational at this point that I can go on for ten minutes and pursue a piece that's not working because I don't want to jump ship yet, because I know there's something in there. Maybe even one sentence for tomorrow night. In the past, I used to get off, or apologize by saying, "Wow, that was unanimous," but now I just slowly move on to something else to bring the level back up. The exception is the time when I'm on a roll, everything's hitting at a high level, and then I try something and there's nothing at all. It's like whiplash to the audience. Then I might say, "Okay, you gotta break these in somewhere."

How did you get into stand-up?

I just backed into it. It was just the next job on the list to get fired from. I was waitressing in a place where they had comics, and I'd sing in between the comics. I would listen to them when I served the food and I realized that I thought exactly like these people. One night they were short a comic, and I was kind of funny around the club, so they asked me if I'd like to go on, and I said, "Sure, I'd do anything to get away from the table yelling, 'more butter, more butter.'"

Was it easy to find your stage rhythm at the beginning?

Oh God, I think I bombed for five years. I only stayed in it because a good friend of mine, Andy Kaufman said, "This is what it's supposed to be. You're in a tunnel, there's a light at the tunnel, and if you don't keep going, you'll end up in the tunnel."

Who are some of your influences?

Buster Keaton, because of his economy. I had a friend once tell me, "If you can't write anything on a particular day, take three extraneous words out of an existing joke, and that'll be your day's work. Don't waste anything." So I'm very conscious of trying to be economical.

Where did you learn about contracts?

I had a lawyer in the beginning who put together a contract, and then when the business started to change and I started to do door deals, I sat down and wrote down every element that I felt was necessary to be covered.

For example?

No personal checks, no cashier's checks, only certified checks, only bank checks always paid before the last performance. Never performing with any monies outstanding. Round-trip tickets so you're not left, mandatory deposit at least thirty days ahead, guarantee that they'll spend "x" amount of dollars on advertising for my appearance. You get no comps, the tickets belong to me—if you want to have guests, you pay me for them. Your club, my tickets. It's hardball and it's ugly and it's horrible every time. It never gets better.

Has it gotten any easier?

No, it's worse because there's so much money coming in and they want it. I say, "Look, you didn't invest in me early on, so you live with the drinks." And they do very well because I bring a lot of notoriety to their club.

Do you have a personal life at all? It seems like you're on the road all the time.

Oh, you can have a personal life on the road, you just have to have it with strangers. Really, I had a four-year relationship, and then I lived with the person after him for seven years. Because you see each other so briefly, it's always like a honeymoon. A quick weekend is so hot. That's the good. But when I'd be off the road for a long time, I'd find out we were mismatched. The bad is that you date the wrong people for a longer amount of time.

You've always strongly resisted being labeled by gender. Why is that?

Once you ghettoize yourself, you're dead. I'm a comic. It's very important to me, and I fight hard. I don't let them write "comedienne" when referring to me. People don't say doctorette, or dentistista, do they? I always did it funny, but I wanted to get the point across. I'm a human being trapped in a woman's body. Most people still think that a woman comedian is Totie Fields and nothing else. That's one of the reasons that I don't do television because the parts they write for women are so bad. They'll bring me something like ugly best friend who can't get laid. I said, "I get laid in life. I see no reason to stop on television." I think that I'm in an entirely different category and I will eventually carve that out. And that's what I hold out for.

Have you ever thought about creating a situation comedy for yourself?

No. That's just a whole other job. It's a day job. A lot of people say it's a natural step, but I say it's not the natural step. Some people have chosen that, some haven't chosen that. The process is so boring. It's all compromise. The lines are never as good as you would write yourself and stand behind. I find it hell to do sitcoms, and I did take a lot of parts to see if I could like it because I know that I could get one. But I don't want one.

Jerry Seinfeld and Roseanne have control of their shows and have crafted their stand-up persona into their shows. Do you think it would be as frustrating for you if you controlled a show, because your type of persona isn't on television?

I just don't enjoy the process of making a sitcom. It just puts me to sleep. I enjoy the process of stand-up, enjoy the process of filmmaking.

When did you find out that you weren't just another comic on the stage, but that people would pay to see you, and how do you feel toward the audience?

I really didn't know until I started to say, "Since we can't agree on a price, why don't I just come in for the door? I think people might come." I was kind of surprised really 'cause I don't have prime-time exposure, and I think the same amount of people who have Showtime are the same amount who voted for Dukakis. As far as the audience is concerned, I agonize if I think that I haven't done a good job. I really want them to leave feeling better than when they came in. That's my goal for the evening. We get so much shit dumped on us in every walk of life that I don't want to throw more shit at people when they're coming to see me.

GEORGE CARLIN
"You Have To Find The Patterns Of Your Thinking"

I first saw George Carlin on the old Ed Sullivan Show in the sixties when he was in his clean-cut, suit-wearing phase. I've always found him funny. But I was truly blown away in 1971 when suddenly he surfaced on television wearing long hair and a beard, doing a more personal and challenging kind of material. It was astoundingly fresh and accurately caught the prevailing zeitgeist of the country. I was a first-year law-school student thinking about being a comedian and remember vividly a routine that George did on The Tonight Show with Johnny Carson about growing up in White Harlem and how white guys who hung out with black guys invariably start talking black. I immediately went out and bought his album George Carlin AM & FM, and listened to it religiously. Along with Richard Pryor and Robert Klein, George Carlin had the most influence on me as an aspiring comedian. His loose, easygoing style, lack of pretense, and social-commentary-oriented material had a great impact on me. In my mind, I used to always associate the phrase "Truth is Beauty, Beauty is Truth" with George, and kept that in the forefront of my mind whenever I was trying to write my material. I also grew a beard, which got me fired from my first job at the Playboy Club in San Francisco. When the club manager called me in and tried to pressure me into shaving my beard, I refused, saying, "George Carlin wears one." A day later George was the only bearded comedian still working in the country.

George Carlin is one of the true giants of stand-up comedy. Still amazingly prolific and passionate about the craft of stand-up after over forty years in the business, he is—most importantly—still funny and relevant. With both Richard Pryor and Robert Klein no longer performing full-time, George is the only one of that great triumvirate still out there bringing his funny, questioning, indignant point of view on a myriad of subjects to the people. He is the keeper of the flame of social-commentary comedy that was started by the great Lenny Bruce, proving that both truth and true hipness are ageless. George was gracious and in fact eager to speak to my class about stand-up comedy in the summer of 1992.

GEORGE CARLIN

How did you first get interested in comedy?

When I was a kid I could make up funny stories about people in my neighborhood, and I could make funny faces and noises. I had that in my toolkit as a kid, and it got me attention and approval. I was good in school, but I didn't really care about that stuff. So I started off in that comedy direction as a little boy. And then there were certain comedians who I was attracted to for the sheer anarchy of what they did, like Spike Jones, where he would take something that was ostensibly beautiful and trash it, and thus force you to look at it with a different attitude. Danny Kaye was another one I liked and, of course, I liked the Marx Brothers for the same reason. I liked Bob Hope, and Red Skelton in the movies. So when I saw them, I thought, "I can do that, so I'm gonna be an actor." To me, acting meant Bob Hope, Danny Kaye, and Red Skelton—not Clark Gable and Jimmy Stewart. And as I got older and locked into my plan, I thought that to be an actor, first I have to be a stand-up comedian in a nightclub. Then I thought to do that I should be a disc jockey first because I'd be the only one in the room and there wouldn't be people who could hassle me, and I could get confident before I started going out on stage.

How did being a disc jockey help you get confident enough for going on stage?

With an audience in front, you're counted on to succeed about every fifteen or twenty seconds, depending on the length of your setup. And you're looking for approval every few seconds, and if several times in a row you don't get it, the dynamic in the room changes. The audience starts getting afraid for you. Working the radio allowed me to get confident about the things that I was saying.

You were part of a comedy team at first, weren't you?

Yes. I formed a team with a funny guy named Jack Burns. My own thinking was that I would move even faster if I was a part of a comedy team. Two guys can work out material faster, and you'll have another guy on stage to share the burden.

Did you get along well?

Yes, we got along very well. We didn't work hard enough, but we were on *The Tonight Show* within six months of forming our act. We moved along very quickly, but we were lazy. But I knew down the line that I wanted to be a single. After two years, we broke up and I was now at the second stage of my plan—which was radio, stand-up, then movie acting. At that time I thought of stand-up as just a stepping stone.

That's interesting because I've always thought that you were one of the few who pursued stand-up for its own sake.

The reason I was able to do that was because of my change in the sixties. Here I was, a stand-up comedian in the sixties. All my life I'd had a feeling of being out of step. I'd been thrown out of three or four schools, I had quit the Air Force, I'd gotten kicked out of the altar boys, the Boy Scouts—anything where there was a lot of authority, I was very soon gone. But I had this dream of getting into the movies, so I assumed that you had to play their game. So there I was in a suit and tie with a mainstream attitude. Around 1967, I broke through on television. I was doing *Merv Griffin, Mike Douglas, The*

Tonight Show, and I got a chance to do some sitcoms. I did a movie with Doris Day, and I did a bunch of screen tests and readings, and I found out that I couldn't act. I had no chops at all. My dream had been shot down. So I said, "Oh, okay. I'll just keep doing what I'm doing." Around this time, all my friends—most of them musicians and street people—had been working their way through the folk movement, and were going into the hippie movement into this thing called the counterculture. And I was still a pot-smoker and listening to rock music and saw that they were using these things that came out of their heart. They were saying what they were thinking about what they saw wrong with the country. And here I was, doing silly things for audiences of older people who were the parents of my friends, and I realized what assholes they were. Thank God for trusting my own gut. I started a transition. First my jacket came off, my hair got a little bit longer, the tie came off. I was still doing television during the transition, but then the breaking point came where I had a few incidents in nightclubs where I provoked the audience, or they provoked me, and it became a scene. I got fired from Las Vegas for saying "shit." And I said, "That's it, now I'm free." I let the hair grow, the beard grow, and starting dressing looser because I wanted to identify with the counterculture.

Was there any fear with such a drastic change?

A certain amount because the unknown is out there, but a great deal of confidence at the bottom of it all because it just felt better. It felt right. And that's why I stayed in comedy so long and developed to the level of proficiency I have because my career didn't allow me to make a lot of compromises.

How do get to be so free in what you say on stage?

I don't care about a lot of things. Personally, I think we're a failed species. I personally root for tornadoes. I hope that the ozone hole gets bigger so that the assholes can get through it. So if you start with that attitude, there's not a lot that they can do to you. You have to start with where your true attitudes and beliefs start.

How have you maintained such a high degree of creativity?

I look at 1988 as a turning point. Not just in getting a good grip on my attitude, but the whole arc of creativity from the impulse coming in and me realizing how it hits my backdrop material, to how to change a sentence that's not working, to how a line needs to maybe be moved to another part of the routine. All that stuff I got better at.

Were you aware of any other counterculture comedians around when you started your change?

Well, the 1950s was when comedy changed forever for the better. Lenny Bruce, Mort Sahl, Dick Gregory, Nichols and May, Jonathan Winters, even Bob Newhart in his suburban way was a departure from what had gone before for stand-ups. And don't forget Lord Buckley, who never had the recognition, and Shelley Berman. Thus, the old order, the Catskills way of playing it safe and avoiding controversial subject, disappeared. I heard my first Lenny Bruce when I was working as a disc jockey in Shreveport, Louisiana, and my life changed. I grew up believing that comedy had certain rules, and Lenny showed that there are no rules. Which is the life I was living anyway. I learned that comedy could say "fuck you" in general. So then I had hope.

Did your parents have any influence on your comedic development?

My mother and father were very gifted verbally. My father was a salesman who could sell you anything. My mother was in advertising. She'd come home from the bus and tell a story about something that happened, and she could do all five characters. She should've been on the stage. I learned from her how you could create a world with your voice.

How do you get your anger out in your comedy?

First of all, I'm lucky that my art allows me to express this anger and dismay. I love human beings one at a time. Individuals are fine, but then they get into groups. And then they have an agenda—which is usually to do something to some other people.

How does a novice comedian develop the type of confident attitude on stage that you have?

The thing that most comedians need to remember when they go on stage is that they're really the boss. But my feeling is that you've gotta believe in yourself, and know what your attitude is and what your observations are based on. There's gotta be a kind of thread to your material because it represents you. It's nice to have a series of unrelated jokes, but it's better when they have a kind of segue. I have always written down everything that I ever thought of—that I thought was worth remembering. When I was in radio, the first year my boss told me, "Write down everything you ever said that you think was worthwhile, because someday you'll be glad you have it." Even if it's just a name. I collect anything that seems to have a larger pool of fellow thoughts. Even though I don't have the other things written down yet. I just keep recording everything I think of.

You seem to walk the line really well of observing a lot of things, but not looking for what's funny in it. You seem to notice something and comment on it.

When I read or think of something, I don't immediately think it's funny, but I become aware that it has a potential for what I call "comic distortion." Something will stand out from the background of the rest of the article and my brain will go to work on it. The mind is a problem-solving, goal-seeking mechanism. I've found that most of the creative work I've done is done on a subconscious level. Just a consistent ruminating. I think that the artist and the scientist parts of the brain have to work together. One side is pointing out to you all these ironies, and the other side has to sort them out and organize them into patterns. That helps the writing, because writing is nothing but the organization of your ideas. You have to find the patterns of your thinking. Like I have thoughts about social concerns, thoughts about little funny wordplay things, thoughts about values that I feel are important in life, and once a month I go through them and read them, and sort them into piles based on their patterns or topics. I find that when I do this sorting out, it helps me see the possibilities for connections. I can see something that relates to something that I might've done the week before. I'll say to myself, "There's a minute there, there's a minute there." And of course that minute can turn into five minutes because by taking that minute and memorizing it, and letting yourself do the jokes in that minute loosely, you can ad-lib around those jokes.

When you're breaking in a new routine, do you have all the thoughts or jokes in it worked out or do you go up on stage with a loose idea?

At the beginning of a bit I have all the jokes, and I know how to tell them, but I don't know how to tell them perfectly. I don't know the exact economically efficient wording that gets me from the beginning of the sentence to the laugh without getting in the audience's way. I know the spirit of the laugh, and how to get to it one way or another, and sometimes in getting to it I'll discover something else that I hadn't thought of so that now the bit is richer, and longer, and I haven't lost the laugh. In fact, I've picked up two more laughs along the way.

How would you describe your performing style?

It's just like being in a living room telling an anecdote to a bunch of friends. I got a good piece of advice when I was working in radio, which was to act like you were talking to one person at a time.

How can a young comedian do challenging or confrontational material to an audience that might not agree with his or her point of view?

There are two ways that I believe that a comedian can make it easier to do confrontational lines. One is to have a tone in the body of what you're saying that keeps it from being solely a hateful screed. The other way, and this is especially important to those who are beginning, is that the audience must see you as non-threatening but authoritative within yourself, and that happens in your first five or ten minutes.

How can someone develop that authoritative air that you have in your delivery?

That comes from the conviction that your thoughts are worth telling somebody. If it's important enough for you to think of, and important enough for you to drive someplace, stand up, and tell people to be quiet so you can tell them about it, that's gotta be in your voice and your delivery.

ELLEN DEGENERES
"If It All Went Away Tomorrow, I'd Have My Life"

Ellen DeGeneres is a clever observational comedian with a distinctly light, offhand style of delivery. Her distinguishing characteristic—apart from the cleverness of her material—is her economical and clear setups. An effective setup is one of the most important tools that a comedian needs for his or her material to be successful because it gives the audience the context necessary for them to enjoy the punchline. Ellen has the ability to give the audience a clear picture of where she wants to take them with just a few well-chosen words.

I first met Ellen in 1986. She opened for me in Las Vegas at The Improv in the Riviera Hotel. I was struck then by her easy, conversational style of delivery, the sly self-effacing spin that she put on her material, and the fact that gender didn't seem to play much of a part in her choice of material. Though she has participated in documentaries, magazine articles, and cable specials that focused on female comedians over the years, her material has stayed distinctly gender-neutral. Her revelations in the last few years about her sexual orientation may have had some bearing on the slant of her material.

Ellen is a very easygoing person with a warm, direct personality, and it was with great pleasure that I invited her to address my class.

At the time of this interview in 1992, Ellen was just about to start her first and short-lived ABC TV show, *Laurie Hill*. She hadn't done her successful show *Ellen* or hosted the Emmy's yet—so Ellen's remarks about the possibility of her someday doing that are particularly insightful.

ELLEN DEGENERES

We worked together at the Riviera Improv in Las Vegas, remember? I'm trying to figure out how many years ago that was.

Is that when we first worked together? I can't remember . . . the fifties.

It was '56.

Let's see. I started in 1983, but I didn't move out here until '86. Could have been about '86.

What's your television show about?

It's not a sitcom. It's more of an adult comedy sort of thing. The first show deals with a child with AIDS. (Laughing) But it gets lighter after that, so don't turn it off.

How do you feel about making the transition from stand-up to actor?

I did a series called *Open House* on Fox a couple of years ago. That was my first acting job. It kind of fell in my lap and happened for me. When I got into comedy, I was just a funny person, and then the more I did it, the more I found my niche and found what I ended up doing was acting. Not like I was a Lily Tomlin. Nothing like that. I don't do characters. But even if it's just one little sentence, if I all of a sudden take that person's character on, I'm acting a little bit. And I just had so much fun doing that on stage that I realized that acting was what I wanted to do. So to me acting is just a natural progression. To me it's just stand-up except, what's hard about it is you get spoiled doing your own stuff, and then all of a sudden you're doing someone else's lines. And you want to go to them and say, "This is really horrible," but you can't do it. Because that's their job, and they're writers and they make their living writing. So, even though I'm not called a writer, I've been writing for ten years.

Can you change lines on the show?

On this show we shot the pilot and I only have like five lines spread out throughout the show. But they did come to me and say, "If you want to change anything, you can." They're great writers, so they don't really need any help.

When you were starting out, did you have a conscious idea of wanting to end up with your own TV show?

No. When I started out, it was that comedy is what it is. I didn't know that this was an option of a career choice. I had no idea that it would be a money-making thing. I was just a fun person and Steve Martin was my idol at the time. I thought Steve Martin was the most brilliant man in the world because he did such ridiculous things, and it had an elegance behind it. He wasn't just this goon on stage doing balloon animals. I thought he was great. I thought that Woody Allen was great.

Did they influence the development of your style?

No. I just saw them on TV and I thought they were funny, but I never studied them and said, This is the way I'm going to do it. I was just basically me on stage.

How did you start?

Some friends were holding a benefit to raise some money. They needed to hire an attorney and didn't have the money, so they were putting a show on. It was like a "let's put a show on in the barn" kind of thing, and they said, "You're funny, why don't you do something funny?" So I just went on stage and told the audience that I hadn't had time to have lunch, and basically ate the entire time. You know how people start to talk, and then take a huge bite, and you have to wait for them to finish that bite, and then they start to say something else, and then take another bite? So I got maybe five words out the entire time I was on stage. I just ate and then said my time's up. That's all I did. And someone saw me and said, "You know, you could play colleges." Then I'm driving one day in the French Quarter and there's a huge sign that says, "Opening soon: Claude's Comedy Corner" just out of nowhere. I'd never been in a comedy club. I went in and I said, "Can I work here?" And they gave me a job as an emcee seven nights a week. I had to play the midnight shows, it was called the X-rated show, and the guy who owned the club tried to force me to do X-rated material, and I said, "I don't do dirty material." He said, "You're going to have to learn to do that." And I said, "I'm not doing it." So I just stuck to what I wanted to do, and if the laughs weren't there, I didn't care.

And that's how you wrote, pretty much on stage? Or did you sit down and write?

No, I wrote every day. I mean, when you start out, you're at the table looking at the salt and pepper going, Okay, what does this salt mean? What does the pepper mean? After a while, it just kind of wears you down, and you don't look at anything like that anymore. But in the beginning, you buy bleach at the store, you go, What's funny about cleaning solvents? You're just going crazy with anything. That's how I wrote constantly.

Was your material like it is now?

I did a lot of prop handling at the beginning. A whole lot of props. And that's so weird because I'm nothing like that now. I had no idea who I was yet.

When did your style change?

When my writing got stronger. When I had stronger bits and felt that I could get laughs from stories and words. I think it's a higher level of comedy. I mean, I like puns and I like visual things, but I just think that there is a higher place to bring it on stage.

How'd you come up with the routine about talking to God on the phone?

A very depressing story: My best friend was killed in a car accident. She was twenty-two years old and this talented writer. I had no money, I'm like sleeping in a basement apartment, fleas all over the place, waking up at night in fleas. And I just thought, "How can she possibly be taken away and fleas exist? What justice is there in this world? I don't understand." And I thought, what would that be like, to pick up the phone and just be able to call and talk to God? I wrote it in ten minutes. I just thought, First he'd make fun of my name because everyone did. Degenerate, you know, and it's just so aggravating. So I just thought of course God would make fun of it. And when I wrote it, I was working places making maybe six dollars a night. Driving twenty, thirty minutes to maybe make six dollars. And when I wrote it, I said, That's going to get me on Carson. That's my first Carson set.

You felt it right then?

I knew it. And that's exactly why Jim McCawley (Associate Producer at *The Tonight Show* at that time) called me over when he saw me at The Improv. He told me that he loved that piece and that Carson would like it.

Has it changed much from the time you first wrote it until now?

It's much better now. I think that my delivery is better. It's smoother.

You take your time and handle silence well. How'd you learn to do that?

I don't know. That's just my style anyway. I just think that you're in control. The audience came to see you, and you don't let them dictate the pace of the show. You set the pace and then they can go along with it. Sometimes you have drunk people who want to yell out when you have those pauses, and that's really aggravating, but the more you stick to it, the people who enjoy that will keep coming back to see you. So you create your own audience and eliminate those with short attention spans.

Does taking your time help you control your audience?

Yes, because if you're nervous, you'll have a tendency to speed up, so I've learned that, no matter how slow you think you're going, go even slower, because it appears that you're in control and not nervous. Then the audience will give you the respect that you're trying to gain from them.

You appear so relaxed when you're on stage, as though you haven't a nervous bone in your body.

Yeah, I come off like I'm not nervous, just because I've learned how to hide it. I used to get so nervous where I felt that it was obvious that I was nervous. I did *The Oprah Winfrey Show* and I just love Oprah so much. I was so nervous that when I walked out, I thought that the mike on my lapel was picking up my heartbeat, because it felt like it was coming out of my chest. And yet, I didn't look nervous.

How have you gotten over being nervous?

Somehow you just learn to deal with it. You learn to handle your nervousness. You just kind of look at it like, you know, you're not doing brain surgery. This is just a wonderful job that you have. And people have paid, gotten dressed, and come out to see you because they want to have a good time. There's always the exception, of course. There's these jerks in the audience who want to mess with you on stage, especially if you're a woman. But now, ninety percent of the time they're there to enjoy themselves. And if you just relax about it, I think that really comes off and the audience has a better time.

How do you deal with hecklers?

It depends on where they're coming from. If they're really being mean, which I don't get anymore because my shows usually cost more money, so it's not like they won it or they already had passes or whatever, so people are not going to spend a lot of money to come to be mean. In the beginning when I had people like that (which I did)—being a woman on stage, you have these macho idiots who are drunk who want to get to you and upset you—they used to upset me all the time. I'd just walk off crying sometimes. I mean, they wouldn't see it, but I would be backstage crying.

So you wouldn't respond back to them?

No. I try not to be mean to people. Unless they really just aren't getting it. Because I just think they just don't know any better. They don't know that it really affects your rhythm and where you are and everything. But usually there are bouncers to take care of that.

How much do you change or play around with an old routine on stage these days?

I'll find a new little area sometimes. I do a lot of long stories, and sometimes I'll find a new line after I've been doing a story, maybe a year, and it'll become one of the killer lines in that routine. But it took me a year to all of a sudden get to that line.

Your transitions between subjects are very smooth. Is that a conscious thing?

I'm really particular about subject matters, and I like to stick to the subject matter blending into the next subject. Say I'm talking about animals and I'll then get into a goldfish thing I do about buying fish for stress, and that they help you to relax and fall asleep, and I go to, "It's just like when I doze off when I'm snorkeling." Or say I'm doing the goldfish piece, and then that takes me into fishing and hunting. Right now I have a new joke that I just put in my act and it's really hard because I have to just stick it in somewhere. And to me, it sticks out like a sore thumb because it doesn't lead anywhere and I have to force it to lead somewhere. That's real hard for me, and that's why it's hard for me to put new stuff in.

Smooth transitions really give a conversational feel to your act.

That's always been really important to me. And it takes a long time. I mean, I've been doing this a long time, and I have this set now, so it's really hard to stray from it just because it is so smooth.

So you're tempted not to change your set?

Yes, and that's kind of dangerous in a sense because people come to see me and they're big fans and they want a really good show, and I feel like if I start messing around with it, taking something out and putting new stuff in, it just really chops it up. So it's kind of a double-edged sword to get so successful.

Do you ever feel trapped into doing old material because it's popular?

Oh yeah. You know, you go through a thing when you're struggling to build strong stuff. Then once you have this really strong stuff, people come specifically to see you and you're worried because you know that they've seen it but then if you don't do it, they say, "Why don't you do that phone-call-to-God thing?" Because they've brought people to see it, or they want to see it live because it was there. But then if somebody comes up after the show and says, "The last time I saw you, you did a lot of the same stuff," it really affects me. A lot. It makes me feel really bad, so I always do try to put new stuff in there. But lately just because I'm at that point now where I'm a little paranoid about it, I'll ask, "How many people are seeing me for the first time?" And it's amazing. At least half the audience, sometimes more than half the audience, is seeing me for the first time. So you've got to make those new fans.

You always seem so spontaneous that I'm surprised to hear how much you set your act.

That's the whole thing. Some people have no idea that you do this over and over again. They really think that it's something that is brand new—and that's the whole secret. You make it fresh, even if they've heard it before. It's really scary when people come back and see me over and over again because I know they know the jokes. But they'll come up to me after a show and tell me that they liked that I delivered a joke a different way so that it's really not the same joke.

Do you write out each routine word for word?

I write every single thing down, because the most important thing to me are the words. I think you need stage presence, I think you need timing, I think you need presentation, but I think content is really, really important. I went through a period where obviously I was just getting to know this, and then I started making money and bought a computer. I thought that it would be easy to keep things in categories, but I just never did it. I write longhand, and I write every single thing out exactly the way it goes. I do it before I perform it on stage, then I play with it on stage, and then once I start playing with it, it's off the paper.

Do you write the way you speak?

I basically write it out how I would say it, or think about it. There was this thing I saw in a Woody Allen movie where they said penguins are monogamous for life. So I wrote that down, because I thought there was just something to that. So I wrote down, Penguins are monogamous for life, which doesn't really surprise me that much because they all look exactly alike. It's not like they're going to meet a better-looking penguin someday. Even if they are cuter, how do you know? And that's all I needed. I thought I needed more than that, but I was wrong. So it's like sometimes you just write down the idea and you don't really need to work any harder than what the idea is.

Once you write a joke, try it out, change it, and polish it, do you put it on tape, write it down, or just remember it?

In the beginning when it was my goal to become a really good comedian, I taped myself every night and wrote when I got back to the condo, or hotel, or wherever I was. I was really thoughtful about it. I'd have a star by something that worked, different things like that.

Are you still that disciplined?

Because I want to get more into acting, I'm not as worried about it and I don't do that anymore. I usually have somebody who travels with me, and they remember what I did that adds something else. Or if it's really, really strong, I'll definitely remember it. I mean, this is what we do for a living, and our egos are not going to let us forget how funny we were at that one moment.

I was watching a tape of your first *Tonight Show* appearance, and I noticed that the audience stopped your set three times with applause for clever lines—which has happened to me as well on TV, but never in clubs. Why do you think TV audiences laugh and applaud, but nightclub audiences will only laugh?

I think that they want to be heard. They know it's your first time, they're at this show, they're excited, they're on TV, they feel like they're almost up there with you.

Your material is pretty angst-free. There's a calm serenity about whatever you're talking about.

Everybody has painful things when they're growing up. I had some painful things to deal with, and I always dealt with it with humor, and that's where my humor was sharpened, but I don't think I come from a real neurotic place. I think everybody thinks that to be a comedian that you have to suffer, but I think it's really important to be happy. If it all went away tomorrow, I'd have my life, and I'd have me. You know, that's what I count on.

Would you speak about being a woman in comedy? What are some of the obstacles that you see?

I don't think anymore that there are any obstacles. I think in the beginning it was harder because there were very few woman, and it was still looked at, like, you should be either singing or taking your clothes off. People—even women—were very intimidated by a woman on stage. I'd be on stage, and I don't even call attention to the fact that I'm a woman on stage. But there are women who were threatened by me, and I could see their boyfriends laughing, and they would be looking at them, and looking at me. Sometimes women are really for you, and sometimes they're against you because you're a woman on stage. But now there's so many women doing it that I think that it's very rare that you're going to have problems. I remember playing a boot camp for like four hundred Marines, and I thought, Gee, they're going to like seeing a woman. And that was a bad thing. They were just screaming out the most obscene things. They didn't even give me a chance to say anything.

How did you feel about that afterward?

You're going to have times like that. It's just that everything builds character, everything makes you stronger, and it's just like life. You just keep training and training and training so that when you're put into the arena, you can perform because you're in shape and you're ready for whatever happens.

Are you ready for everything now?

Yeah, as far as stand-up and stuff. The second time I did the *Comedy Awards*, they asked me to talk for a few minutes and explain the judging and stuff. And I had to walk out and stand at the podium and there's Lily Tomlin, Steve Martin, Penny Marshall, and all these people in the audience that I'm just in awe of, and I had to talk and try to be funny in front of these people who have seen everything. And I just kept telling myself, This is training for when I host the Oscars or when I host the Emmys or when I win an Emmy. You have to look at everything as though it's getting you ready. And you're getting closer and closer each time.

RICHARD JENI
"You're Trying To Paint A Picture"

Richard Jeni has an act that is rapid-fire. Rapid-fire thoughts, ideas, and images, all flowing from a machine-gun intelligence. A well-aimed stand-up M1. A comedic Martin Scorcese, Rich has one of the faster deliveries in comedy, but his enunciation is very distinct and clear. Using sound effects to great effect in his act, as well as employing imaginative physicality and a strongly skeptical and questioning point of view, Rich enhances his routines with a variety of comedic elements. When I called him and asked if he would consent to talking about his craft, he said, "Gladly, I can talk about comedy for hours." This interview was conducted October 10, 1996, at Buzz Cafe on Sunset Boulevard.

RICHARD JENI

I watched your stand-up specials, and one of the things that caught my attention was how much you physically animate your routines. Is that instinctive or something you consciously try to do?

I don't know if it's so much instinctive as it was a result of noticing how much the audience likes it when you physicalize it, because really what you're doing when you do comedy is you're trying to paint a picture in somebody's mind. And the more vivid the picture is, the better chance you have of getting them to laugh at your idea. It's like the difference between a book and a movie. What's fucking me up is that I just realized that I still don't think of myself as a performer first. I think of myself more as a writer. That's always been my orientation, and physicalizing things is really just a way of servicing the idea. It's only in the last year or so that I've actually started to enjoy the process of figuring out how to perform things. It was always sort of a necessary chore: part of the job, a question of, How can I perform this?

Did you ever have a stint where you were a writer exclusively before you got into stand-up?

No, but any success that I ever had in school or on jobs was based on my ability to write things better than a lot of people could. I was always good with words. I don't come from performing. I was never even a mushroom in a high-school play. I had never been on a stage before I did stand-up comedy. So my orientation was not that of a performer. That was something I had to learn. I was basically a wise-guy class clown. A guy with a good mouthpiece and an ability to work with language. And I still don't consider performing the strongest part of what I do, but my ability to perform is starting to catch up with my ability to write. As you know, there are a lot of comedians out there who have almost no jokes, but yet they're very successful and the audience likes them because they can make a face or do a voice. To me that's a joke. A joke is anything you do up there that gets a laugh.

I'm surprised that you don't consider yourself a strong performer because when I watched your specials, your relaxation and command of the stage gives a totally different impression. I've watched a lot of stand-up specials and I haven't seen a lot that were anywhere as well performed or gave the impression that the comic was as completely at home on stage as you. Are you as at home on stage as you appear?

I feel more at home there than a lot of other places because, ironically, what appears to most people to be a scary situation isn't. If you know what you're doing and the audience is inclined to laugh, which they are, the situation can't vary that much. Since there are very definite parameters, you don't have what makes most things scary, which is the unknown. I mean, everyone understands that it's your show, not their show, and the deal is I'm gonna talk, and you're gonna listen, and if I'm funny you'll laugh. Once you know what you're doing, and once you've seen it go well nine hundred times in a row, you start to get comfortable that this thing is not gonna vary that much. Whereas in other situations, say interpersonal situations, anything can happen.

How long has it taken you to get to this place? How long have you been doing stand-up?

Fourteen years.

Were you that comfortable when you first got on stage?

I sucked. The whole first year I was quitting every day. I'd go to guys and say, "Do you think I should be doing this, because I suck and the audience doesn't like me?" In reality I just wanted reassurance because I really wasn't quitting because I had no-where to go.

Were you getting laughs?

No. I was pretty bad for the first year.

Were you getting no laughs, or sporadic laughs?

I would get laughs here and there, but I was kind of flailing, trying all these different approaches that had nothing to do with me. Steve Martin was real popular then, and I thought, That's the way to go—we've seen enough observational comedy and I'm gonna go all the way out.

Did you have props?

I had a couple props and other embarrassing things that I used to do. When you're trying to be experimental at the beginning, it's al-most the worst time to do that because the audiences you have are terrible. They're small, drunk, hostile, and they have no respect for the show because it's usually someplace that doesn't inspire respect, like the back of a Japanese restaurant. It's like you're trying to pull off the hardest things when you have the least amount of skill. So I didn't make any money the first year.

Where did you start?

I started out in Brooklyn, in Pip's, a small coffeehouse-type place in Sheepshead Bay.

What gave you the courage to even try and become a comedian? I imagine that you were the class clown, right?

I hate to even say this because it's such a stereotypical story, but basically I knew I wasn't gonna be on the football team, and I knew I wasn't gonna be a big ladies' man, and I wasn't gonna be the toughest guy in the school. So what are you gonna work? You're gonna work the brain angle. I don't know if I'd call it courage; I'd call it desperation. I had learned to get acceptance from people because I was funny. I learned I could hang around with kids seventeen and eighteen when I was twelve as sort of a mascot because I could make 'em laugh. Also, I felt a strong attachment to my father, who was a funny guy in a very sarcastic, witty, quiet sort of way. Not a guy who was gonna be the life of the party, but if you were around him a lot, you would see the wit. My father had an interest in comedy. He had a lot of comedy albums from the old nightclub days: people like Jackie Cannon, Belle Barth. When my parents weren't around, I'd play these records. And they were dirty, and naughty, and I'd think, Wow, this is just the coolest, most grown-up thing. So basically me getting interested in comedy was a way of imitating my father's behavior. But if I'd only had my father around, I would have never become a comedian, because my father is very introverted, bordering on a misanthropic personality. My mother was a different personality: very pretty, liked to party, and for a little while even flirted with having a singing career. So I think I got the inclination toward comedy from my dad, and the ability to bond with people, or perform, from my mom.

Do they come see your shows?

They do now. My mom used to come right away, but my father didn't come until he was sure that he wasn't gonna be humiliated. He held out for about a year and a half. I prefer that they don't come anyway.

Why?

Here's the problem with your parents coming to see you: A guy like me doesn't do a "character" act where I put on different clothes and make-up. I'm basically doing me, but it's not really me. It's me to the tenth power—an overexaggerated, overconfident version of who I am, and it's hard to maintain that illusion and image of yourself when the people who changed your diapers are two feet away. It's like having your mom walk in when you're having sex.

Has that ever happened to you?

No, but it's the same type of psychology. It just makes the job of turning yourself into something else more difficult.

You say for the first year you tried all types of approaches to being a comedian. How long was it before you zeroed in on your essence, or persona, that you have now?

I don't know if I've even zeroed in on it yet. It's an elusive thing. It's like the minute you catch it, you're sort of past it. I'd say I've zeroed in on it in the sense that I'm not consciously trying to do anybody else. At the beginning, I was consciously trying to do Steve Martin, and after that I was consciously trying to do Richard Pryor. He was my big epiphany. I saw Richard Pryor at nineteen, and that changed my whole view of what stand-up was. I'd never seen anything that funny in my life. I didn't know that existed. I'd always seen stand-up comedy on television, and I always liked it, but I never saw anybody do it that way.

Are influences important to the development of a stand-up comedian?

If a young comedian is really trying never to be influenced, I think they're doing themself a disservice. Would you be a novelist and say, "I'm deliberately not going to read any of the great books"? Would you be a scientist and say, "I don't want to know what anybody else is working on"? In one sense there is no real truly original idea. All you have is a set of preexisting ideas combined and filtered through you.

How many years was it before your own point of view became clearer?

I was never really conscious of having a point of view. What I was conscious of the whole time was the question of, How can I get as many laughs as possible as close together as I can? So at the beginning of the career, you're driven by getting work. And the way to get work is to keep being reliable. And that gets around. So the first five years I was just conscious of trying to get a foothold in the business and I wasn't so much concerned with the quality of it. My yardstick was, What would I laugh at if I were in the audience? For a while I went through a period where I wouldn't say any dirty words. I wouldn't even say *ass*. And the idea of that was that if you have to say *ass*, *shit*, or *fuck*, then obviously that joke isn't that good, and you're not doing that job. I did about a year of that.

Was it harder?

Yes, it's definitely harder when you have that rule. But then one day I said, Why am I knocking myself out like this, because it dawned on me that when I'm in the audience as an audience member, the guys I like tend to be a little bit bawdy. So I was holding the audience up to a higher standard than I hold myself. And if you start doing that, saying you won't say this or that word, or that topic, it's like a pianist who starts ripping some of the keys off the piano. There's nothing wrong with being dirty, or filthy, or provocative, and there are people better than me in other fields who aren't above that. In the service of a larger point, you can be disgusting, or maybe use profanity just as a guilty pleasure. There's things in my act that I know aren't great pieces of humor, but I feel that if you establish that you don't have to go low, then you can go low for a couple of minutes just as a fun thing.

There's a stream-of-conscious quality to your act. How much of your nightly act is consistent versus writing on stage or just going with the flow?

I would say on any given night, ninety percent of it is pre-planned.

Same order?

No. That's the thing that changes. Your act is sort of always evolving and fluid. But it's usually gonna begin in one of two ways at any given time, and it's gonna end in one of two ways. It's the stuff in the middle that's up for grabs. It's like you're a magician with a bag of tricks based on what the audience is responding to or the mood that you're in.

Can your mood determine what you're going to do on a variety of shows? How bored or fresh you feel about a routine?

Yes, and especially on the road, my physical condition. As you know, between the flying and the getting up early to do the radio shows, sometimes it's a chore just to get through the show without falling on your face. And in most cases, I can say that I only have "x" amount of energy to get to the finish line, so I pace myself. Say like at a club where you have to do three shows on a Saturday night. Now the seven o' clock people don't know it, but I'm not putting everything out on the seven o'clock show, 'cause I know that I'm gonna be on stage a total of three hours, and I also know that the seven o' clock people are the least drunk and the least tired and so you don't have to come out and smack 'em around as much as you're gonna have to smack around the midnight crowd. So that seven o' clock show's gonna be a little slower paced, a little less walking than I usually do. I look at a couple of bits: "Well that one's a lot of work, a lotta running and yelling. Maybe we'll save that one for the later show."

What are your writing methods like?

I'll jot down ideas for jokes, and so I'll have these little ideas for jokes laying all around the place. When I'm in a mode of actually writing for one thing or another, I might make an effort a couple times a week to actually sit for a few hours and deal with them. If I've got other projects going on, then I'm going up on stage just to stay limber, and maybe a joke'll come. Maybe it won't. One of the problems of writing comedy is that you have to limber up and you're not limbered up so to speak. That's why I've found that one of the most productive times to write, if you can keep from chasing the local women, is after the show.

Why?

Because everything is charged in that direction. All those comedy switches are on.

Do you tape your shows?

If I have a specific thing coming up, if I'm consciously trying to develop new material or make old material better, yes. But, I'm not always in that mode. When I had that TV series, I just went out on the road to make some money and have some fun. I'll have a period where I've just done a comedy special that I've been working on for a year. I might want to coast for a while. Kinda bask in the afterglow. But when I'm trying to develop new material, it's absolutely crucial for me to tape.

Were you the type who would work three or four sets a night when you were starting?

I started out in the fifty-dollars-a-night gigs around New Jersey and Long Island. I was afraid to go into the big clubs in the city for a couple years. I broke it in on the road, and then kinda brought it to Broadway, so to speak. In retrospect, I think that was a very good idea, because if you start out in the clubs, there's a tremendous amount of pressure to play to the comics in the back of the room. Or to play to whatever the prevailing idea of good comedy is at that time. And at that time, the idea of good comedy was to be a monologist, and hopefully a Jewish monologist. That point of view. A lot of the people who were getting the most work in New York at that time were Jewish men or women who had sort of a neurotic, sarcastic approach—even a similar delivery, which they used to call the "comic-strip shuffle." A kinda hybrid of Robert Klein. So you'd have to be too much of that person—instead of your own person—if you were in that environment.

So you were avoiding being influenced and thus getting to your own individuality without knowing it?

There's a good and a bad to that. The good is that, you're more on your own and you're not being influenced. And the bad is you're more on you own, and you're not being influenced—because the better comedians were in Catch a Rising Star, The Comic Strip, and The Improv. They weren't out at Mustache Pete's in New Jersey. So I didn't get to learn from the people who were really good.

How did you develop your audio and sound effects? Elephants, conch shells: You're one of the few stand-up comics who does them.

It's like Tang coming out of the space program—an unintended effect from going for something else. I would consciously try to make things more vivid, and in the process of saying, "Women going shopping is like a primitive ritual," make the image more vivid. My favorite book is *Lord of the Flies*, and the leader had the conch shell, and when I think of a primitive ritual, my mind flies to the blowing of the conch shell. So when I started talking about women shopping in big packs—which is based on experience as a shoe salesman— that led me to the analogy of it's like a primitive ritual, which led me to thinking about primitive rituals, which led me to thinking about *Lord of the Flies*, which led me to the conch shell, and then one night out of an accident on stage, out came this noise. I didn't sit at home practicing it. I didn't start out as a guy doing a lot of voices and sounds. The thing that is really interesting: I couldn't do a lot of these things when I first started out, and one of the reasons that I couldn't do them was because I didn't believe that I could do them. But as time went on, I started to be able to do them, and as I started to get more confident that I could, I started to try more, and started to succeed—to where I end up today where you're asking me how I do all these voices and sounds. Research has shown that the more you use certain parts of your brain, the more neural connections are made to do that.

Do you practice those types of sound and vocal effects now or do you just go with an impulse when on stage?

I'm never really consciously trying to figure out what kind of sound I can make. I still start off in my mind with, What am I trying to say? What's this bit about and how can I service it? It's like you're a painter, you want to paint a picture of whatever, and then you start thinking about colors and brushstrokes and composition and all that stuff. I start off with, Here's a thing that I think is worth talking about. How can I bring it to life for the audience? If some things I do didn't have a sound effect in them or an impression or a physicalization, they wouldn't be worth doing because they wouldn't be that funny. I do other routines that don't have any of those things but can exist on their own because of good lines, or as a good piece of timing.

What do you see as your greatest strength as a comedian?

I always felt that whatever success I've had as a comedian is because I don't do any one thing great. But I do a lot of things pretty good, and it adds up to a whole that's greater than the sum of its parts.

Is the acceptance you have these days a boon to your creativity?

Absolutely, no question, because you don't have to convince them. It's a more nurturing environment, and to the extent that you feel the audience likes you, it makes you feel more relaxed, and to the extent that you feel relaxed, I think that makes you more creative.

How do you feel your education helps you with your comedy if at all?

I think it helps in the sense that it makes you aware of a lot more information, and the information is pretty much the clay of a monology act. The more connections you can make to topics and ideas, the better. For example, I read *Lord of the Flies* in college, and it wound up influencing a bit many years later. So the more things you know about, the more raw material you have.

In reading your bio, I noticed that you majored in Political Science, yet there's very little politics in your humor. Why?

I don't talk about politics that much because the stuff that people laugh at the most are things that they relate to on an emotional level. For most people, politics is not an emotional issue. It's stuff they read about in the paper. For that reason, when you go into those areas, it's hard to get a strong reaction. And the other thing about politics is that it's extremely complicated to the point that the politicians don't even understand the issues that they're dealing with.

Bill Maher does a lot of humor on political and cultural issues because he says that those are some of his main interests. Have you found that you don't do political humor because it's not one of your strong interests anymore?

Yes, I have lost interest because I realize that politics isn't about what's right or wrong about the country anymore, it's about the game of politics—the show. Nowadays people watch politics the way they watch sports. The pundits are like sportscasters. They're just keeping score and telling you who won today, so on that level it doesn't interest me, because when you're doing stand-up, there's always the imperative of the joke. You've gotta be funny a lot in a short amount of time, and if you talk about politics and social issues in a meaningful way it takes too long. So all the jokes end up, "Bob Dole is old; and Clinton can't keep it in his pants." To me, those jokes aren't morally superior to a joke about a 7-Eleven.

Have you had a good joke just stop working?

That very rarely happens to me because I try to design my routines with longevity in mind, so I don't venture into a lot of stuff that's going to have a short shelf life. Like the other night, I thought about doing a couple of things about Dole, but I decided that I didn't want to bother with it because it's a lot of work, and a month from now, there'll be no Dole. But if on occasion a joke suddenly stops working, it's either because the audience is bored with the topic because they've heard that topic too much, or you've become bored with a piece of material and don't perform it as well as you used to. Sometimes I'll over-tinker with a routine past the point of improving it. It's not broke, but I'll break it anyway.

JAY LENO

"Comedy Doesn't Come From Inflicting Pain..."

I first met Jay in 1973 in Boston while playing a club on Boylston Street called Paul's Mall—a fact I'd forgotten till Jay reminded me at this interview. My first comedy album was out then, and I was making a tour of the East Coast, playing folk clubs to promote it. In those early years, we both worked The Comedy Store in Los Angeles (where I used to call him Mr. Chin) and developed a long-lasting friendship and great mutual respect for each other's approach to stand-up comedy. Then as now, Jay was always neurosis-free and able to take the many disappointments and misguided "nos" that we performers get in show business with an amazing equanimity and determination to just continue what he was doing. I remember his equally good-natured wife, Mavis, once telling me that whenever Jay would get rejected for a project, all he would say was that it was just gonna take a little longer. During the eighties he became a legend among comedians and club owners because of his indefatigable work ethic, acerbically funny material, and the enormous responses he would generate from audiences. Oft times I'd come to a club a week or two after Jay and have a club owner wax ecstatically about both the great business Jay did and what a pleasure it was to deal with his genuine good nature. Jay once told me that he operated under the act-check philosophy: "Do the act, pick up the check," he said. Of course, with his stature, it's obviously been check-act for many years now. Despite having no pretensions at all to artistry, he has emerged as a blue-collar comedic artist with his sharp intellect, dedication to truth, and work ethic.

Of all the talk shows that I've done, Jay has been the only host who would come to your dressing room before the show to put you at ease. In a business notorious for people saying one thing to your face while thinking another, with Jay, what you see is what you get—a straight-talking, straight-shooting man. His word is his bond, and that has never changed, no matter how successful he's gotten. The moment I'll always remember in our friendship occurred in 1984. I had been on the road for a while and arrived in Lake Tahoe to work a casino. By coincidence, Jay was working at another hotel. At that time, not being anywhere near as non-neurotic as Jay and given to periods of introspective self-indulgence, I was feeling depressed about the travel and my career. After my show, I went over to see him and started talking about quitting. Jay just wouldn't hear of it, and that night he and Mavis talked to me for hours, trying to lift my spirits and encouraging me to continue doing what I was doing.

Because of Jay's simplistic approach to stand-up, and life in general, he was initially reluctant to talk about his stand-up comedy techniques, feeling that there was nothing to be said. I prevailed by telling him that even if he felt that way, it needed to be said—aspiring comedians who were fans would be interested in what he honestly felt. When I arrived at his modest office at *The Tonight Show*, Jay was wearing his blue-denim workshirt and jeans and going over jokes for the special six-minute monologue he was doing each night during the Olympics. This interview was conducted at Jay's office on July 31, 1996.

JAY LENO

So Jay, how long we known each other now?

Twenty-five years.

Is it twenty-five?

I met you at Paul's Mall [a now-defunct Boston club] when you had that album with you holding the popcorn on it.

Actually, it was an Ajax can.

Oh, right. And I remember we sat out on the porch of the house I had on Hollywood Boulevard, and talked about Springsteen being on the cover of *Time* and *Newsweek* at the same time. That was '74.

You started in Boston, right?

Yep, I was in a comedy group for a while, but that wasn't very successful, because the trouble with an improv group is, like with anything else, you have some guys who wanna work all the time, some guys don't want to work at all—some guys want to take vacations. So I just broke off and started doing a single.

Did you bomb much when you started out?

I was really fortunate in that before I played a real club—Lenny's on the Turnpike, a jazz club in Boston—I worked strip joints.

What made you go to strip joints?

Primarily because there weren't any others. You're talking '69, '70, and strip joints were the offshoot of vaudeville. There weren't any comedy clubs. You had these folk hootenanny clubs and strip joints. And most of these strip joints would have some bad comedian emcee who would fill in while the girls were changing. Most of them had three or four performers, and although I was bad, there was always enough noise in the room to justify to myself that I was doing okay. It wasn't until I worked at Lenny's with Buddy Rich that I walked out to a room that was silent and listened.

Do you remember the first routines you did?

The first joke I did was that silly hot-plate routine about not being able to have a hot-plate in your dorm room—how you could have drugs, you could have sex, but you couldn't have a hot-plate. I had a lot of bad jokes for the strip clubs, like "that new male deodorant Umpire for men with foul balls." Just bad, stupid stuff. The one thing I learned very quickly was that your material will ascend or descend to the level of the room that you are playing. And when you went into a jazz club, you realized that you quickly better ascend above the normal cut and thrust. If you stayed in a strip joint, you wound up with an act that those people understood, but you couldn't go anything political. To me, when you talk about angst, I remember working in the mid-seventies with these black acts who were caught in that window of time where they had an act they had done for years, which was essentially a pandering kind of act because they had to work white clubs, but they were angry at themselves for doing the material. You know, something like, "I'm not really colored, it's just the lights in the club are very bright." And you'd look at the performer and if it was an all-white audience, they could kind of live with that, but if they scanned the room and saw that one black guy sitting there, it would bother them. And that's the way I got when I would work the strip joints. I had this sort of bad, semi-dirty act.

Did you use profanity?

Oh yeah, early on. Nothing that you couldn't replace. I have no problem with obscenity, it's just that one time a person said to me, "You're not dirty enough to be a dirty comic, and you're not quite clean enough to work this room for big money, so make up your mind." And I realized that I always liked clever wordplay, and I always liked someone who could come up with a clever twist that you figured out was an obscenity rather than actually saying it. The exceptions were people who were clever like Pryor, but when I watch some of these *Def Comedy Jam* shows, I'm not shocked or offended, I'm just bored.

I would never have become a comedian if I hadn't seen Richard Pryor on my twenty-first birthday at the Redd Foxx Club.

The people who did that for me were Robert Klein, David Steinberg, and, to a certain extent, George Carlin. I remember a lady up the street said, "You can't become a comedian unless your father was a comedian. They have a union." Show business is one of those rare businesses where people who know nothing about it feel free to give advice. So Klein, Steinberg, and Carlin were the first comedians I saw under forty who weren't poor, or lower-eastside, and had things I could relate to. Klein was a guy who's dad was like mine. Same thing with Carlin. I've always liked comedians who you could not tell were comedians by looking at them. Like Johnny Carson, Jack Benny. I never liked the wacky-clothes-with-a-big-cigar-and-a-funny hat comedian.

Do you ad-lib a lot in your shows?

I don't know how it works for other comedians, but I have the ability to recall anything in my life that ever got a funny reaction. People ask me if I can remember the first woman I had sex with, and I go, "I have no idea, but I can remember the first thing I ever said that was funny."

What was the first thing you ever said that was funny?

I was in the fourth grade and it was the first joke I ever told that was an adult-style joke. It was about Robin Hood and Friar Tuck. The teacher was talking about how the Sheriff of Nottingham was very mean, and if he caught outlaws, they would be boiled in oil. And I said it couldn't happen to Tuck. And when the teacher said why, I said because he was a fryer. And the teacher said, "That's enough of that." But for the next couple of days I'd be walking in the hall and other teachers would ask me what I'd said in Mrs. Allen's class.

I've always felt that the goal of a stand-up is to get to the point where you are the exact same as when you were your funniest, say with friends or in high school.

Exactly. It took me a long time. I'm almost there with *The Tonight Show*. It takes a long time before they know your personality.

Were you a good student in school?

No, not at all. I never missed a day at school, but my thing was if I just pay attention, I should be able to get through this. I remember I was in the fourth grade and kinda just staring out the window and the teacher said, "Jay, do you think you're a good listener?" And I said, "No, I'm a terrible listener. I was just looking out the window and thinking about something." And the teacher went, "Oh well, you fooled me. I thought the way you were looking at me and nodding, you were paying attention." I remember thinking, I'm never going to do that again. Here I had her totally buffaloed.

What was your process of writing material?

To this day, I don't have a joke file. I have nothing written down. I just do the jokes and throw 'em away.

Then how do you keep track of your material?

I just keep it in my head. The good jokes I remember, the bad ones I forget.

That's amazing. There's no neurosis in your comedy, which is interesting since a lot of comedians and people in general these days seem to have these troubled childhoods.

I didn't have any of that. No problems at all. I was a show-offy kind of kid. But I think it's because I have the ability to identify with the people in the audience rather than the people on stage. I'm amazed when I hear people refer to themselves in the third person. Show business is a bit like a compliment. Somebody says you look nice, you say thank you and you leave it at that. Because when you have the ability to do that, when they say you suck, you can have that roll off your back as well. We have a whole publicity department here at NBC that they pay thousands of dollars to say nice things about you, and the stuff is so professionally done that if you pick it up and read it, you could actually start to believe it. But of course it's not true. You have to have some objectivity. Like when I leave work, and leave the jokes, I go to my garage and I screw around. But I see other people who leave show business, then they go to another part of show business. So their whole life depends on how they do in show business. If I have a bad day here and I go in my garage and physically fix something, then I'm proud of myself for accomplishing at least one task that I feel good about that day.

Was your comedic point of view clearly established in your own mind when you started out or did it evolve?

It takes a while to do that, and I think that I got away from that for a while on *The Tonight Show* and now I can get back into that again.

Why did that happen?

Too jokey. Too comfortable. I think the thing with the new Letterman show helped. To me, the real comedy comes when you become the picked-upon person instead of the person on top. This is what I always hated about Andrew Dice Clay's act. I knew Andrew before, and I always thought he was an okay guy, but I hated his act because he came from the wrong point of view. He was the majority. My grandfather used to tell me that when he came off the boat, the Irish cops would stand there and bang the nightsticks on the dock, waiting for the Italians and then just beat the hell out of them just for getting off the boat. In Andrew Dice Clay's act, he was the cop. And to me, to be the comedian, you have to be the guy getting hit on the head. Comedy doesn't come from inflicting pain, it comes from getting pain. That's why I go out on the road, that's why I like to talk to the audiences.

You're still doing comedy dates on the weekends. Why do you do that after a full week of shows?

I've always looked at my act as the principal and television as the interest, and as much as I like doing television, I realize that to do television, I need 125 people. To do my act I don't need anybody, I just have to show up. I can always make as much money doing my act as I can doing television. So between the two of them, it's fine. In the dark days when it was like, "Oh Jay gonna be fired and replaced by Letterman," I'd go out on the road and play a 3,000-seat auditorium. There'd be 3,000 people there, so I'd know I'm doing something right. I'd go, "Okay, obviously it's not all little numbers on a piece of paper and demos—somebody's laughing at this. It just clears my head. To me, doing my act is the same as going to the gym, or somebody else running. It just reinforces that you can do this again. Most comedians will tell you that your act is really your best friend. It pays for the food, it heats the house, it introduces you to women. It's your best friend. I've always told comedians that if you can do this for seven years, I mean physically make it to the stage for seven years, you'll always make a living. If you've been in the business longer than seven years and you're not successful, there's probably another reason. Sex, dope, alcohol, drugs—you just couldn't physically get to the stage. Sam Kinison is sort of an example. He was funny, hilarious, but near the end he couldn't get to the stage anymore. No matter how popular you are, promoters are not going to rehire you if you miss gigs.

Why seven years?

Because for most comedians it's like college. You study for four years at The Comedy Store or The Improv, you start to get paid at the end of the fourth or fifth year—I mean paid in terms of here's $500 dollars for one night, not $15 or $20 for a set. Then by your fifth or sixth year, you're rolling. You're opening for a big act or playing Vegas, and doing okay.

I think the thing that has struck me most both then and now is the simplicity of your approach to being an entertainer, in that you're virtually angst-free.

I think that's because my interests lie outside show business. Like if you work on cars and motorcycles and hang around people who are not in show business, you get more of a feel for what it takes to earn the money you make in show business. I had a guest on the show one time, and during the commercial break he said he wanted to ask me about what type of sports car he should get. So I told him that the new Ferrari is pretty neat. And he said, "Yeah, but everybody's got a Ferrari." I said, "Don't ever repeat that statement in public. There are car enthusiasts in the Midwest who've never even seen one on the street." Recently I got in a discussion with a writer from Vanity Fair who said that he had heard that Letterman had re-signed for $16 million a year, and asked if that bothered me because I make like half that. And I said no, my deal is based on what I need to make me happy. I can't spend all the money I make.

Are you a workaholic?

No, but you have to understand that I went through most of my life not being able to do anything particularly well. I wasn't any good at sports, I wasn't very good at anything, and my main problem was that when I did something, I would always be thinking of something else. Like when I was in school, I'd be thinking about being out of school. My attention span was short. Whereas when I got on stage, that was the first time that I did something where I did and thought about it at the same time. That was the only time that I was ever focused, and it's still true today.

Did it surprise you to find that you could focus on stage?

Yeah. I did a few episodic things and they gave me a script to memorize, which I did, but doing *The Tonight Show* is the exact same thing that I do anyway. You know, sitting at a deli, sitting at a club, sitting with a comic throwing lines. That's what my job is now. So it's not really work to me.

You've been doing this twenty-five years and you're still prolific as a joke writer. Do you feel you have endless creativity?

I think you have to be interested in being a comedian. There's a lot of comedians who want to be a comedian so they can get an acting job or a sitcom, not because they want to become a comedian. But if you asked me if I'd rather be a comedian or The Tonight Show host, I'd be out of here tomorrow if I had to make a choice. I never wanted to be a TV personality; I don't want to be known as a broadcaster. Some people say to me I'm not a very good broadcaster, and I say fine. I'm not a broadcaster, I'm a comedian who happens to be on TV. I can always keep my house, feed my family, and pay my bills with my act.

Jay, how do you stay so grounded?

I was never a good fighter. At school I got into a couple of fights and always got beat badly, and I use that as sort of my gauge. Say I see I guy who I couldn't beat up when I was young. Now I'm rich, now I'm famous, but I know I still can't beat up that guy. But there are people in show business who think now that they're rich and famous that they can. But you can't. You are no better than you were before, you're just richer and famous. The thing about comedy is that you don't wield any power with comedy, you just reinforce what people already believe. You can't change anybody's mind. The classic example of that is the joke I used to do about Reagan where I say that he had come out against the electric chair, and people in the audience are going, "What?" Then I would continue by saying that because there are so many people on death row, he wants electric bleachers. Then the crowd goes, "Oh yeah, that's what I believe already." You take them one place, but then you bring them right back to where they are. If you try to change their mind, you're no longer a comedian, then you're a humorist, then you're a satirist, then you're out of show business.

Comedian, humorist, and satirist to me can be the same thing. It's just a deeper look, isn't it?

Listen, most people lead lives that are so dreary and mundane. Like if you're a cop, or a nurse, or if you have some job where you just see the worst part of society, all you want to do when you come to a club is laugh. You don't want some little rich-kid comedian come out there and tell you why you're an asshole, or why your problems don't matter.

When we started, Klein, Carlin, and Pryor were doing challenging material that also made you think as well as laugh. Do you really think that people don't want to think when they're being entertained?

No, no, no. Don't get me wrong, but what is the overriding thing about the guys you just named?

They're funny.

Exactly. The good comedians always put the jokes above anything else. To me, the ideal joke is when you've got your stupid redneck over here and your college professor over here, and they both laugh at the same joke for different reasons. The professor is laughing because it's clever and sees that you might mean something else, and the redneck is laughing at the obvious.

What do you look for in a comedian for *The Tonight Show*?

I look at performance, and I look at material. The idea being is that if the material is weak, the performance will carry you through. And if the performance is weak, the material will carry you through. So if you have both, you have two back-ups. A lot of times you'll have guys who have good jokes, but they'll stand in one spot, and unless they write as well as Steven Wright, that joke'll fall. But if they can perform by doing a funny face or funny movement, that'll save it.

Are comedians born? Is it totally instinctive?

I think it's instinctual, 'cause that's where the drive comes from. If you don't have the drive, then it's never gonna happen. If there's something else you'd rather do, you'll probably go do that.

RICHARD LEWIS
"I Just Open My Mouth"

To me, Richard Lewis is one of the modern comedians whose comedic mind has genius capabilities. I find myself continually surprised by the absurd, surrealistic images and associations he conjures up during his frenetic presentation. He is definitely a stylist who doesn't appeal to everybody's tastes because of his acts nervous intensity. Through his many cable specials and television appearances, Richard has developed a persona of a man dressed in all black consumed by constant angst and neurosis that people think is an act. But it's not. That is Richard.

I had the opportunity to spend eight weeks working with Richard in 1987 on the movie *The Wrong Guys*—which turned out to be the wrong movie. It was shown on airplanes three weeks after it was released in 1988. During the filming, Richard was a man in turmoil. He was breaking up with a girlfriend and writing a script in addition to acting in the film. Richard was not a happy man. He was going through a very introspective time and was reluctant to conduct an interview for quite a while. Near the end of the shoot, we returned to Los Angeles, and he was more relaxed and agreed to be interviewed. This first part was conducted in 1987.

RICHARD LEWIS

One of the things I want to talk to you about is your influences. Was there someone who influenced you stylistically?

Not consciously. I mean, it took me a few years to get my own rhythm down and it became close to how I talk in real life. And then, unfortunately, all my problems came out on stage, and it's been a nightmare ever since.

Well, you do perform a very personal act.

It's very personal. I'd like to do your personality or anyone else's. I'd like to go out and just do Art Carney. But I can't.

There are comedians whose material stays away from anything in their own life. Does mining your personal traumas for material take its toll on you?

It might take a toll, but there's no other route. I mean, I couldn't go out on stage and express someone else's feelings. It would have made no sense. So it just worked out this way and I've spent a lot of money on many therapists since I started performing.

Is the self-expression cathartic for you?

It's very cathartic. Just doing what you want to do in life is cathartic. Then the craft starts taking its toll and you lose some of the pleasure. It ebbs and flows. Some years I'm into it, and some years I'm into other things or trying to write scripts—I lose the interest to work on stand-up. I'm starting to get a bug for it again the last few weeks.

How long have you been doing stand-up?

Sixteen years. I came in when it was a nicer environment, when Robert Klein, David Brenner, Jimmy Walker, and Steve Landesberg and those guys were working around.

In New York?

Yeah. We used to hang out together, help each other. But now there's like millions of comics and it's just—it's more lonely.

You feel that it is?

It's more lonely to start out. Back then, there weren't as many comics and it was more fun.

It's like the way they talk about the tennis tour now. The old-timers say that they would not be on the tennis tour right now because, even though there was less money then, there was more camaraderie.

Right. There's pros and cons with it all: There are more places to work, there are more opportunities and more money to be made, but I'm just saying aesthetically it was sweeter—you really felt like you were with the chosen few just getting on stage. Now people who are set decorators wanna do stand-up.

Everyone I know views going into stand-up as being something that's very courageous, something hard to do. How do you feel about that?

To me it wasn't. I had no choice. For me fixing a light bulb on a ladder is courageous. But generally speaking, in a show-biz sense, stand-up is tough 'cause having to make different people's sensibilities all come in unison on one thought successfully is tough. So, it's a tough end of the business, but it doesn't take courage to do it, personally. Not if you're good.

How do you prepare for a performance? Like say, the last fifteen minutes before you go on, what's running through your head?

I've always brought my notes on stage with me because I have so many images in one set and because of my need to have new material all the time.

Has that always been a strong drive?

It's the only drive I basically have had in the last five or six years. Other than to make a living, which I guess is a drive too. I prepare—depending on the type of gig it is—by looking over mounds and mounds of new material and finally culling it down into one concert. And then I bring my torah up on stage with me and apologize for the first five minutes and they allow me.

I thought that was just something you did at The Improv.

No. Even in my specials I brought it up.

Do you get any negative feedback about that?

Never, and I wouldn't care. It's the way I work, and people who come and see me don't care either.

So there really are no rules to stand-up when you think about it?

Not if you make them laugh.

Do you still have anxiety before a performance?

I always have anxiety, mainly because I want to be good, and I'm always afraid—you never know, a relative might sneak in and heckle me or something. So, I worry about things that could happen.

Are you hard and critical on yourself?

I've got a whole jury with me in my chest.

How do you feel about stardom? You've achieved a certain amount of it. Is that a drive?

Not for stardom. Whatever recognition I've gotten—primarily through the *David Letterman* show—I've earned and I feel great about it.

You don't ever seem to have creative block or writer's block when it comes to material. Is that an accurate perception?

It's accurate only because I never sit down with the purpose of writing. I always carry pads with me and I have since the first day I started, thinking I was a lunatic for writing a joke down . . . like what am I doing? I do it the same way as I did sixteen years ago. So, I have a backlog of material, most of which I haven't even worked out yet on stage, but I found funny enough to type on a piece of paper. Fortunately, I can look through these pages before major gigs or TV shows.

Do you ever play it safe? Do you ever say to yourself, I really don't feel like breaking in something new tonight because this old stuff is working very well, or does your boredom force you to deal with something new each show?

When I'm working The Improv, I always do new stuff. Maybe not the whole show, but the majority of it. When I'm doing a paid concert, I still bring up this sheet that has a tremendous amount of new material—and it all depends on how many times I've gone over it how much of it I'll try. It's a lot of pressure to do that with the lights on you and a lot of people in the audience. But I always at least have the sheet at my disposal. Otherwise I feel I'm wasting my time.

Do you feel that the perception of comedians being more temperamental than the average person is true?

I don't think so. I think, if anything, comedians are more easy-going. It's like saying our drug problems are only indigenous to sports people. It's the same thing. There are some psychotically obnoxious comedians, and there's some really genuinely nice ones.

It's just that in every book I've ever read about comedy, we're always lumped together as being these depressed people.

Oh, depressed, I didn't hear that word. We are singularly the most depressed group of people in the world.

Why?

Because I feel we need too much attention, we're babies, we're introverted, we're convoluted.

Would you characterize yourself as introverted?

I can be. Like a lot of comics, we can be on and feel accepted, and other times we go into a shell and want to shoot people.

It's like an extreme, isn't it? Richard Pryor to me was always a study in extremes. He'd either be very up and loud or very quiet. No middle ground.

I used to be that way. No more. Now my depression is more equally distributed during the day.

What is the source of your depression? You're a bright, successful, good-looking guy.

That's something I spent years trying to figure out. I wouldn't even pretend to answer it in one sentence. But just, you know, the search for self-esteem. That's the key.

You're known as having developed a kind of a neurotic persona.

It's true. I am neurotic.

What is the neurosis?

It's unnecessary worry. Like I'm worried that this chair is going to break while we're having this interview, and most people wouldn't. I worry about a lot of things like that. I worry that you'll misquote me and I'll have to call the Mafia.

How do you turn your mind off?

I don't really turn it off very much. I don't know how. That pretty much sums up my total pain. The only time I'm totally relaxed is when I'm in the shower or on the toilet. And then I wind up thinking of jokes . . . so I'm only relaxed maybe ten seconds.

Any hobbies?

Friendship, movies, reading. I'm a sports fan. That helps me. But no fishing, no skiing, no crafts . . . I don't make ashtrays or go in the woods and shoot a deer in the head.

Are you a comic or a comedian?

A comedian.

What's the difference?

It's the definition I once heard: A comedian says funny things, a comic says things funny—oh wait, it's the other way around. Well, I'm doing it in Hebrew because it's a Jewish holiday. Like a comic can get laughs just because he has funny lines. A comedian is getting laughs for himself. And if he's lucky enough to have good lines, he's in.

How do you turn on your funny side?

I just open my mouth, you know.

● ● ● ● ●

This second interview was conducted outdoors at the Buzz Cafe on Sunset Boulevard in July of 1996. It was a temperate, sunny, smog-free day, and Richard was in a mellow mood that matched the weather. He seemed refreshed by his hiatus from stand-up and his subsequent decision to return to it. Dressed in his trademark black T-shirt and slacks, even the little bit of angst he displayed was sunny.

Richard, the last time we were together was on the set of *The Wrong Guys* and you were breaking up with a woman whose name began with an N. Nurit, I think.

I don't know anyone by that name anymore. I'm the Kafka of comedians. I've gone out with an M and an L, and a J. I've gone out with the whole alphabet, man.

Did you do a Z?

Yeah, she was a stripper near the airport. Zenya. No, I'm just joking.

You're doing stand-up comedy again for the first time in two years. Was there any particular reason you gave it up?

I didn't have a really good significant other, and being on the road without being able to call someone who really loves and cares for you takes its toll. Without having that loved one and child, I said, I'm losing my passion, I'm burned out, and my health suffered. So I took two years off.

You were doing pretty well at the time, weren't you?

Yeah, seventeen years into my craft, I was lucky enough to be doing some gig and Jamie Lee Curtis was looking for a co-star and I
got the gig and did four years. All of a sudden, seventy million people
knew me who otherwise would not have. Which enabled me to do
3,000-seaters in Carnegie Hall, and specials whenever I wanted. I
was lucky enough that, because of the show and all that work, I
could say, I'm just going to get my act together. And I did. I took
about a year and a half off, but I never stopped writing.

What did you write?

I would write a journal.

You have a daily journal?

Yeah, like a Kerouac kind of deal, but without being grandiose, I
just write jokes. I wrote other types of stuff, but—

**Is it just ruminations, or are you really consciously trying to write
material?**

No, I write stand-up material all the time. So I have thousands and
thousands of pages. So what I do is never repeat one line ever on
any show I ever do because I have a record of it. Every Leno, every
Letterman.

On your TV shows, you mean.

And every special.

But not your concerts?

No, in concerts, I change every three months primarily. It's almost
a new hour.

Every three months you have a new hour?

At least. Yeah.

Wow, that's awesome. That's an amazing amount of turnover. What causes this creative restlessness?

It gets kinda boring to me. That's why I like acting in films, because once it's done, it's done, and you move on. Like, right now, I'm working on a new HBO special called the Magical Misery concert.

Let's see, you've done *I'm in Pain, I'm Exhausted, I'm Doomed*. What's this, the sunshine series of concerts?

I never said I was the New Christy Minstrels of comedy, man.

How'd you come up with the latest title?

I asked Ringo Starr, who I know and call Richard (which is his real name). I said, "Richard, I'm thinking of going back on stage, and I'm scared, and a little miserable about having to do it again, but I think I want to do it. I'm thinking of calling it the Magical Misery Tour, to parody the Magical Mystery Tour. You think I have to ask Paul and George?" I felt like such a jerk. I mean, these cats are worth $500 billion, like they give a shit. And he says, "I doubt it."

That's all he said?

Yeah, he laughed. He just slapped me five and said, "Do whatever you want."

Is the hour you're creating for this special as strong as you feel it can be?

Not yet, but it's getting there.

Describe your process for getting your material ready for your special.

I'll try to be as succinct as I can. I'm doing my fourth special this Christmas, or Hanukkah, or if there's an Islamic holiday. I'm an equal-opportunity religious cat. But I'm sure I left out a few religions, too. Anyway, the deal is this: I was looking at my notes, and I had about four and a half, five hours of stand-up material. So I went away for about two weeks, and I boiled it down to three hours of stuff that made me laugh. So I put it on my yellow sheet of paper, which I bring on every stage, be it The Improv or Vegas or Carnegie Hall, just because it's new. And I always bring on like twice as much material as I'll ever use. But the deal is I go on the road for like six months solid.

You'll go for six months straight?

No, I'll come back periodically, but then I'll start figuring out what's getting laughs, and what isn't, so by the time I hit the Bottom Line [a club in New York] and tape it for HBO, I'm going to be really sure what's cooking on stage. And once this Magical Misery concert is done, I will never do that material again. I just like to get it documented. I've been doing this twenty-six years, and I feel very proud to have an archive at Ohio State University [Lewis's alma mater] where they keep everything I've ever done.

Everything?

Yeah. See, I never had this notion that I was going to do this forever.

Stand-up?

Yeah, whatever—be in the arts. It took me a long time to make money doing it, but I never wanted to do anything else. So I kept everything. If I was on a local show like *Good Morning, Dallas*, I have the cassette. I always asked the producer to deliver the cassette to the hotel. So I have thousands of cassettes of everything I've done. Every *Letterman*, every *Tonight Show*, all my sitcom stuff. Every silly appearance I've ever made. The dopey ones, the good ones. So it's interesting to see your growth.

That's true, isn't it? It's like an A show from when you started out would be an F show today.

I don't even consider it an F show because it's as good as I could have been then.

Sure. I understand that. Did you grade your early shows?

Yeah, I put B, D, and I'd save the As.

What would you grade your shows on?

Number of laughs and audience response mainly.

Was it tough to get laughs when you started out?

David Brenner—who's like a brother to me—once told me, "Richard, why do you want to go on stage at The Improv, the most important showcase in New York, with new material for the first time?" So he gave me names of clubs, forty miles out of the city, and he says, "Take about six months." So after six months, I went to open-mike night at The Improv and I blew the roof off because I was so ready. And I was watching people going on for the first time, and you could tell that I was working on my craft and they weren't. And it was only because Brenner gave me that advice. He also told me that if you do a joke in front of 20,000 people and you just hear a titter, get it out of the act. That made me laugh.

When you were starting out, were you aware that you were developing a craft. I mean, you come from an educated background. You were a copywriter, right?

Yeah, I went to college. A middle-class family. And then I became broke as soon as I graduated college.

Really?

Yeah. I had a lot of jobs. I worked at The Museum of Modern Art. I worked at sporting-goods stores. I sold stuff door-to-door.

Did being a copywriter help you with the craft of writing jokes?

No, not at all. Copywriting just got me depressed. Though there is a craft to writing jokes. For example, if you listen to Woody Allen's albums, every joke is a gem. They're structured and the punchline comes pretty close to the end of the line. He was certainly one of the best at it.

Why did you choose a small club like The Bottom Line for your HBO special when you can draw so many more people? It seems almost like going back to your roots.

Yeah, I'm going back to the village where I started because the premise for this special is that this is my last show ever.

Do you feel that?

No. I don't think so. I've been getting the passion back. The shows have been cooking. But in this special, I want to sort of make it a little organic and say to my manager, who will be played by an actor, "This is it, I've done it twenty-six years, I want to go back to where I started, so if this is it, I want to finish where I started. Because I'm digging acting and writing."

To complete the circle?

Right. *Siddhartha*, man.

Did you read *Siddhartha*?

Of course I read *Siddhartha*.

Hesse's *Narcissus and Goldmund* is the one I liked.

I only got to Narcissus, and then I fell asleep. I'm saving the *Glass Bead Game* until—

That's a hard one.

I'm hip. My friends said to me, "Read it just before you die." That's the advice you got in the sixties. Nine out of ten people I asked for advice in the sixties were probably doing mescaline. "Read it on your deathbed." Thanks, man.

Was it tough to get the passion for stand-up back?

It took about five or six months to get it back, because after two and a half, three years, you're a little rusty. So you start to feel you don't have it.

That long? What kept you doing it when it wasn't coming back?

I had no choice. I'd spent two, three years in movies that were not pushing my career. Like, for example, I had a ball working with Mel Brooks in *Robin Hood*, but being in a parody of Robin Hood wasn't going to get me a role with Marty Scorcese. So I had to say, with the advice of management, Why don't you go back and do what you do pretty uniquely for yourself? And I just couldn't go out and do two gigs and come home and then go back three months later to another nightclub. See, I had this theory, I said, I did Carnegie Hall eight or nine years ago, and I want to see if I still have fans. You know, you get that paranoia. But I needed to do a lot of shows. And the only way you can do a lot of shows is to play nightclubs. And two shows a night are murder at my age. I used to do three. So I decided to charge a higher cover price and see if Richard Lewis fans will actually come to the nightclubs to get the room mainly filled with people who would come to see me in a concert hall. And it worked.

Was it your idea or your manager's?

Both, but I wouldn't call this a profound idea up there with the Theory of Relativity.

I think it's higher than that. There's a Pulitzer Prize for career development, and the Nobel committee is considering adding a category for ticket prices.

Anyway, it worked ninety-five percent of the time.

Mostly fans came in, and you had good houses?

They came in, because they had to pay to come in. It was more than just a "Saturday night, let's go to the club and have a two-drink minimum."

It became a conscious choice?

Exactly. I wanted to know if my material would work with my fans, not just with anybody who would come to any nightclub.

I've always been fascinated with that large list of material you bring on stage. Does that mean you don't depend on memory?

No, I do.

Tell me how, because you can always consult the list.

The list basically has about twenty categories. So if there's a category, say, sexual performance or low self-esteem, I know underneath that category I will have twenty or twenty-five jokes. It reminds me of what I've prepared, but I need to look down because it's new.

So you just have the categories, not the actual funny lines?

No, I'll have, say, a joke about masturbation. That will be the category, and under that, I'll have maybe fifteen jokes. But before I get to that sheet, I'll have looked over thousands of lines about masturbation—literally—and narrowed it down to the twenty I love, and that's what's on the sheet. So when I bring it on stage, I'll glance at it. I was a good back-court player; I've got good peripheral vi-sion. Just for a second, I'll see masturbation, low self-esteem, take a sip of coffee, take the mike, and I've got twenty masturbation jokes rolling off my tongue.

Do you have your concentration from the minute you hit the stage, or does it take a while?

I'll ad-lib in the beginning. It's like, if you're in Dallas one night and Denver another, and the night before in Denver there was an avalanche, you've got to deal with it. I need a couple of minutes to look at the environment, and if there's like triplets sitting in the front row, I'd be a moron not to talk about triplets, and then get off on maybe some kind of riff. Plus, I love ad-libbing.

You do a great deal of ad-libbing?

Oh, always. I write a lot of material. That's why I hate doing it, but I have to listen to every tape.

You tape every show?

Every show. Ever since I started. Robert Klein was a great inspira-tion to me in that regard. He's one of the reasons I got into the business, because I realized that you can be intelligent, and be on television.

Stand-up comedy up until the sixties was more vaudevillian than intelligent, wouldn't you say?

It wasn't like the other comics weren't intelligent. It's just that their brand of humor didn't play that well on television. It was very broad and it wasn't as intellectual as Allen, Newhart, Win-ters, Cosby, Sahl, Berman, Pryor, Nichols and May, and Lenny Bruce, of course.

They became the intelligent comedy vanguard?

No question about it. That was the new wave. Like the new wave of cinema in France. Like Truffaut's *The 400 Blows* in 1959. It's pretty much the same era.

If you hadn't seen that type of humor, do you still think you would have become a comedian?

Yes, I would have become a comedian because I was writing jokes for other people. But I was getting rejected on all the lines I found funny. So I ultimately got on stage to do what I wanted. Those other people gave me, unconsciously perhaps, confidence that, if I just follow my heart, and I'm any good, I'll make a living at this.

Did you bomb initially, and how did you handle it?

I'll show you a microcosm of show business, which is a roller coaster. The night I went to The Improv to try to become a regular on open-mike night, I went on at 8:30. I was there with my college sweetheart, and I blew the roof off. This was like after six months of prepping to do this night. And Budd Friedman comes on stage, puts his arm around me, and says, "Hey man, you're the new Rookie of the Year." Anyway, after I made it that night, I should have taken my girlfriend out to dinner and said, "I'm a regular at The Improv, man, with Robert Klein and David Brenner and Jimmy Walker and then Freddie Prinze," bless his soul, but I got a little cocky.

You went to do another set?

No, Budd says, "You want to be on the regular show?" I went, "Hey, of course, man." Seven hours later at three a.m. with three drunk pirates having intercourse in the front row, I bombed. And I drive home with my girlfriend feeling like a piece of shit.

Was the feeling like, now you've got up to the big leagues and you can't cut it?

No, it wasn't that. The audience was drained from eight to two. They'd already seen Klein do an hour and a half, Brenner, Landesberg, Rodney, Pryor on occasion came—so everyone knows that if you go on after thirty-five comics, you could be the messiah and go, "I have the flu, I'm going to take a pass tonight." That is if you're hip enough to know that the room is burned out.

You think the messiah would be that hip?

He'd better be. Because, you know, *Clockwork Orange* is a sitcom now. But when I drove home that night, I wasn't in touch with that reality, and when I went to bed, I felt badly because all I remembered were the four or five people, with their heads on the table, and I wasn't wise enough to know that it wasn't a "comedy room" anymore. When I performed the set seven hours earlier, it was a room filled with fresh faces who wanted to laugh. And that was like a microcosm of what the business is like. Disappointment, and then the phone rings. "Really? I got that gig?" That first night was symbolic of what the business is forever.

How long did it take you to get back on stage?

First of all, I had a girlfriend. She pointed out that it was two in the morning, and that there were four drunks in the audience. She put some perspective on it. So I got right back on stage.

How long will you stay with a joke that you think is funny but is not getting a reaction from audiences?

I don't know an arbitrary number, but after four or five times delivering it the same way in front of a pretty good audience who has come to see me, if I don't get a big laugh, then I'm pretty clear about it—if it's funny to me and not to the audience, it's out of the act. But the interesting thing is sometimes I'll do an esoteric line on television that won't get a laugh, but it will get a laugh for the people who are going to pay to see me in concert. Because I know people are lying in bed and they're hearing this hip line and they go, Hey, he's coming to town and he did that joke about Kafka playing gin with one of the Wright brothers. I'd rather sneak it in on television than do it on stage if it doesn't get a laugh. And it's less painful to sneak it in on television than to have 2,000 people stare at you in an audience.

What's your attitude toward doing television appearances?

David Brenner once said that if you do one *Tonight Show* to eight or nine million people, more people will see you in eight minutes than if you did The Improv every Saturday night for 400,000 years to a full house. So I treat every TV show like it's a Super Bowl, short of putting charcoal under my eyes.

How do you adapt your act for doing panel on, say, *The Tonight Show* or *Letterman*?

I rarely do my act on panel.

What do you do on panels then?

I mean, I've got the bangers in my head.

Bangers?

Bangers is the euphemism for stuff I've done on stage that I know gets laughs, but I give this advice: I feel panel is an opportunity for people who watch TV to get to know you as a person. That's where you should be more personal in my belief. My material's personal anyway, so it blends.

You once told me that before the *Letterman* show came out, you didn't feel that you had a forum. Was that a frustrating time?

Yeah. I though about quitting stand-up then because I felt that I didn't have a chance to be as good as I could be on any TV show regularly . . . to have an audience. Doing *Letterman* was very cool because he said, "You're better just sitting down and wailing." Whereas my early Carson shots were hit and miss, because I'm very physical on stage and it's not good for the camera. If you're very physical, it looks almost amateurish. I didn't panel with Johnny until I got my sitcom with Jamie Lee because he insisted that comedians do stand-up. So some shots went well, and some didn't, because I need to get warmed up. You once told me after a set at The Improv that I reminded you of a jazz guy. You said that my comedy riffs are very jazzy.

Yeah, I remember. I said like a saxophone.

Yeah, and that really meant a lot to me because I'm a big fan of yours. But that was the thing. I needed that time to warm up. I needed to do my scales for three minutes, and then all of a sudden on TV, it's good night, and I hadn't got into my stuff yet. That's why I never do stand-up on television anymore.

How long a show are you doing each night now?

It depends. I go over an hour if the audience is cooking. But because I talk so fast, over an hour is too much on the audience. If you're doing a concert in front of two or three thousand people, an hour and a half I don't feel is an abuse, but if you're doing a nightclub, an hour is tops, and that's enough, man.

Are you as funny now as you used to be before you became a comedian?

I feel the last hour I've been as funny as I've ever been in my entire life. And you weren't even interviewing me. I was alone, just talking to myself. Now, I'm like Ingmar Bergman with sneakers on, and I apologize.

BILL MAHER
"This Is Wrong, This Is Out Of Place, and I'm Gonna Shout About It"

Bill Maher has always been a comedian interested in commenting on the many substantive issues affecting—and sometimes infecting—our society. Extremely well-versed on the many issues of the day, his stand-up has the tone of a witty lecture filled with literate, acerbic, social commentary lamenting the death of common sense in the country. This restless intellectual questioning culminated in the perfect forum for his concerns in his popular cultural-discussion show, *Politically Incorrect*.

Politically Incorrect caught fire by capitalizing on the fact that an increasing number of thinking Americans had become uncomfortable with the fact that free speech on "touchy" cultural, racial, and political issues in this country was slowly being eradicated under the supposedly enlightened doctrine of political correctness—a specious doctrine that presupposes that just because something offensive isn't said, it isn't being thought. Rather than acquiesce to this doctrine, Bill decided that it's better to have an intelligent discussion of certain—as he likes to call them—"rude but true" beliefs and philosophies held by people than to deny people the right to express them. What is particularly interesting about Bill Maher's stand-up act and television show is to watch this intellectual Peck's bad boy, who doesn't suffer fools gladly, get genuinely indignant about what he feels is a nonsensical point of view or cultural icon, and respond immediately from his gut without censoring himself, only to then realize that he has espoused a unconventional and controversial viewpoint, and find himself peering down from a provocative high wire.

In July of 1996, I was doing a benefit stand-up appearance at The Comedy Store for CARE, and Bill was also a performer on the show. He had just come from taping *Politically Incorrect*, and yet, he was visibly nervous backstage while waiting to go on. I was somewhat surprised and commented on his nervousness that night at the start of our interview, which was conducted at the *Politically Incorrect* office on July 26, 1996.

BILL MAHER

The other night at the benefit at The Comedy Store, I was surprised at how nervous you were before your performance.

I've never felt comfortable at The Comedy Store. I've never worked there; it's not a room that I know.

Was it because of the room itself, or because you hadn't done stand-up in a while?

I do stand-up a lot. I go on every weekend.

So the room itself had that effect on you?

Yeah, because when I started out, there was The Comedy Store and The Improv, and I couldn't get on at The Comedy Store. I never had a comfort zone there, and I guess it was still in my head. You know how intuitive we are about rooms and the different vibes.

I never really noticed the differences in rooms that way. I'd do the John Wooden thing and just play my own game, so to speak. I got a little nervous early in my career, changing between black and white audiences because I'd have to change material.

I don't know that experience specifically, but I certainly know the feeling of changing your act a lot for two different audiences. Like one night I'm at a college, the next night I'm doing a corporate gig, which is hugely different. Whenever I have a gig coming up, I always have my assistant make me up a card showing who's going to be in the audience: Is this a suit-and-tie gig, how old they are, do they want me to work clean? All those things make a huge difference.

You've always had substance to your act. Tell me a bit about how you started.

I started in 1979 in New York. Catch a Rising Star was my main club. There were only three: Catch, The Improv, and The Comic Strip, and I worked them all. Catch was really my home, though, and it's the club that I was talking about in the novel I wrote about that time. I lined up on a Monday night like everybody else, and then spent that first awful year just trying to get on. I think the first year is just the hardest. If you can get through that, the rest is downhill.

Did you bomb much the first year?

Of course. I mean, how can you not bomb the first year? I don't know how anyone can get laughs even the fiftieth time. I don't know when was the first time I did a set where I actually got fifteen minutes of decent laughs, and felt something like a comedian, but I'm sure it was at least a year into it.

What were your writing methods like when you started?

I remember back in New York when all the young comics used to have these discussions comparing techniques about writing, and I tried every trick to sort of write on purpose and it never happened. Eventually, I'd just keep little scraps of paper and jot down things I'd just say in conversation or think. As long as I was good about jotting it down, and I'm good about that, I'll go through things down the road and put it somewhere where it makes some sense and is funny. I'm pretty good at gathering notes.

Were you disciplined at the beginning?

I certainly had my difficulties getting down to the grindstone in comedy, because when you start out, it's very hard to be inspired to work on your act because you're bad, you haven't gotten good yet, and every time you go on stage it's a sucky experience. So who wants to go home and work on your act then? It also works the other way. If you do good, you can be inspired to work on it.

Do you remember the first routine you wrote that got really good laughs?

There's a routine that I've never done on an HBO special about Swedish mothers giving birth, and how their names sound so guttural. It's like they give the name as they're giving birth. OLAF!!!

In school, were you known as a funny person?

I thought I was pretty funny in school. I wasn't the class clown or anything like that. I made my friends laugh and enjoyed being whatever it was I was trying to be—witty I guess. I made the teachers laugh more than the kids. I wasn't trying to buck authority and get the teachers mad, I was trying to get the teachers laughing. Teachers are looking as much for relief from the tedium as the kids.

Did you find yourself drawn to watching comedians as a kid?

Yes. I watched Ed Sullivan. I watched Alan King and Robert Klein. I think Robert Klein was a big influence on a lot of people of my generation, just because he was like the first of that new breed. Carlin too. In those days there just weren't that many comedians. Anybody who was a comedian, you knew about. There was a time when I thought Klein was just untouchable. I remember listening to his albums and transcribing some of his bits word-for-word so that I could see it on the paper. And I discovered that I could never do his style because he would say a punchline three different ways. It was kind of sloppy, but it worked for him.

Even though Klein seems to be mentioned more often as an influence than Carlin, George is more of a presence in the public's mind as a stand-up than Klein.

That's because I think George remained more dedicated to the stand-up craft.

Were there artistic influences other than comedians on your approach to comedy?

Dean Martin.

Are you serious?

I know he's not thought of as a comedian, but I remember his show and I thought the world of him. I always liked Hef and Dean. I guess when you're an adolescent boy—and that part has never left me—I still think Rat Packy. It's campy, but it's cool. I like Bing Crosby—anyone who has that super-relaxed style—and Dean was the best.

So you're the Dean Martin of political humor?

Hey, you should see me late at night at my house when I pull out the smoking jacket.

You own a smoking jacket?

Several. My friends used to say, "Oh good, we're gonna get Heffed up." You should see it, it's . . . fly.

Is anger necessary for good comedy?

No, but it is for mine. Everybody has a different style. As a fan, I'm going to go see *The Cable Guy* with Jim Carrey. There's no anger there. But he makes me laugh, and I'm glad he does. But for me as a comedian, there's gotta be an element of, "This is wrong, this is out of place, and I'm gonna shout about it."

Sometimes my friends will say that I'm very funny when I'm really angry. And I'm not even trying to be funny. It's really weird.

Right. There is a close alliance between anger and humor.

Have you ever been working clubs and found that a routine that was working suddenly stops working for no reason?

Yeah, that's a funny phenomenon. The joke sorta like goes away. That's why I tape every set because sometimes it's just the delicacy of how you do it. You do it almost the exact same way, and it's a completely different result. It really depends on very, very minute things in there that either give the audience just enough information—or maybe too much information—before the punchline so that it's not a surprise. Whatever it is, it's still a mystery to me when a bit goes away. Also, I think an audience can sense when you're excited about it and it's new to you. Sometimes you're not thinking about why it's funny anymore because that's gone away for you. You have to get back into what you loved about it to begin with, so that you're not just reciting words that you've said before.

I've found that sometimes you have to just put a routine away for a while.

I do, too. And then you come back to it and it's fresh again. A lot of times it's also what you put it with. A bit that won't really work well can find a companion piece that will make them both work fabulously well.

Do you always listen to the tapes of your shows?

Sometime the show is so much fun and you feel like you've done so much new stuff that you want to listen to the tape immediately. Even if I don't listen to the tape right away, I try to go over my notes, see what I did, and try to remember all the things I do want to listen for, so in case I don't get to that tape for a month I'll have notes about it. Like if I don't remember the exact wording of something that's crucial, I'll know where to find it.

You keep all your tapes or do you tape over them?

No, I used to tape over all of them, but now if there's something good, I'll just keep it.

Do you move your routines around a lot in your act?

Yes. I realized something this year when I was going out every weekend to do stand-up after working a full week here, and people were asking me why was I killing myself: This is really my hobby. I mean, what is a hobby? It's something you really enjoy working on after you get home from work, and this show is really my job. And it's also something that you do on the weekends. I'm working toward December when I do this next HBO special, and I will have had basically a year to put together a whole new hour, and I think I'm right on schedule, but it is a lot of work putting the bits together. You get a rough outline, then it becomes clearer. Now I have so much of an outline that whatever new thing I get, I know generally where it's gonna go—I'll think this will go well in this section.

You enjoy the structuring process?

I really do. I really enjoy putting the puzzle together. And being able to put together an hour in a year is a great satisfaction because it took me ten years to get my first hour of material.

Does a change in lifestyle affect your ability to come up with material?

Yes. I believe it does. Especially as a comedian, you want to be in touch with as much as you can with everyday life, and the more successful you get, the more you become removed. You sit in first class, you ride in limousines, you don't do your own shopping. That's all bad for a comedian.

Is that why your humor both in your stand-up and your show is more of a cultural overview of the news than a personal revelation?

You've got to work from what your life is, and some of that for me will always be what is going on in the newspaper, which is so much bigger than what's going on in my life. But it's also how you relate to it that's important. I'll talk about the budget-cutting going on in Washington, and then I'll talk about going to the mall and seeing all the stores selling unnecessary shit, so do we really need to be cutting the budget? I try to bring the hi-falutin' political down to the level of where it actually hits you. I would rather see a comedian say nothing than try to have the audience relate to their relationships with movie stars, and their problems with ten-million-dollar divorce settlements. Some of the subjects I've seen comedians talk about I literally get offended at. I don't think that is what comedians should be talking about. Comedy is about what you and the audience can relate to, and if all you can talk about is your hi-falutin' life, then you shouldn't be doing stand-up anymore.

Did you have big ambitions early on?

When I was old enough to stay up and watch *The Tonight Show*, I realized that I didn't want to be like any of the comedians that were on it, so much as I wanted to be the man. I mean, I could see who was City Hall, and who was trying to get into City Hall. And Johnny was City Hall. As soon as I saw Johnny Carson, I thought "Oh, that's a good job, I wouldn't mind doing that." I was eleven or twelve years old then, and I'm forty now, so we're talking almost thirty years.

And you've never wavered from that goal?

There was one major time when I got away from that, which was when I got out here and started to make my living as an actor, when I thought, I guess I won't be Johnny Carson, I'm gonna be something else. But I still continued with my stand-up. It's funny how that career direction went away, and then it came back. I guess it was supposed to be on my track.

Do you think that if you had acted in a show that became a hit, you would've let stand-up go?

Not stand-up, but I probably wouldn't have gotten into talk shows.

You were doing stand-up, and you were doing sitcoms. What made you decide to do a show like *Politically Incorrect*?

I had thought for a long time that it would be a good thing to do. I think a lot of it was timing. Not just business timing—as in the right moment in the business to do it—but also the right moment in your life when you are seasoned enough, and well-versed enough, and have a big enough, deep enough bag of tricks. Because that's what you need to do a TV show every day, and that's what you get after all those years on the road.

But also a timing that corresponds to a certain mood of a segment of the public?

Well, you hope it is. I guess it means that most nights you're tapping into the right stuff.

Do you get many letters?

Yes I do. I'm sure I get a lot less that *ER*, but I have trouble keeping up with it. But I read them all.

How intelligent are your letters?

I'm sure I don't get as much mail as some shows, but the quality of it is very high. Some of it is pure fan mail asking for an autograph or a picture, and I love that. I've worked enough years to not feel guilty about enjoying that kind of basic recognition. But I also get a lot of mail from people who watch the show and want to engage me on an issue, and they often educate me on something. There's a lot of bright people out there.

You have to do a monologue every day. How's the adjustment from writing your material to having to depend on writers?

I still write my material for my act, but a talk-show opening monologue is a different beast. It's right out of the day's headlines. It's very perishable. I rarely use anything from this show in my act, and even then I've retooled it in some way. It's also a very different rhythm. To me it's the difference between doing this [Bill leans forward in my direction] and doing this [Bill stands very erect with a backward bias]. With my stand-up, I've got the mike in my hand, and I'm prowling and working, and taking it to them. My show monologue is standing on the corner commenting on the parade that went by today. It's drier.

As a result of the success of *Politically Incorrect* you're playing bigger venues now. Do you have to make adjustments in your delivery?

Not really. The only adjustment I had was learning that after all the years of struggle I'd be that anxious to get back on road. Not only do I enjoy the putting together of the material puzzle, I also enjoy delivering it. More than ever by far.

Is acceptance an important factor?

Yes it is. They know what to expect. You don't feel like you have to prove yourself. Your type of comedy is not a surprise to anyone who might have expected Gallagher. The audience is there to hear you and what you're thinking. Now, it's really like talking to a bunch of friends. At least, that's the way I feel about it.

PAUL REISER

"I Allow Myself The Freedom . . ."

Paul Reiser is a comedian whose delivery is idiosyncratic and slightly reminiscent of a gentle, well-adjusted Woody Allen (who is one of his influences). And like Allen, Paul is interested in the nuances of interpersonal relationships. A classically trained pianist as well as an excellent actor, Paul successfully translated his relationship and marital concerns from his stand-up act into the sharply observed, long-running NBC situation comedy *Mad About You*. He also wrote the music theme for the show, and feels that some of the principles of playing music can be applied to performing stand-up comedy. This question-and-answer session was conducted at my class during the summer of 1992.

PAUL REISER

How old were you when you first starting going on stage, and where did you start?

The first time I ever went up on stage was when I was seventeen, and I did it once. But I went back to college and it was, "What did you do with your summer?" and I said I was a comedian. I was a comedian for like five minutes. It was so good to say, though. But I really got started at Catch a Rising Star, literally on audition nights. You'd wait in line from four in the afternoon and get a number, and you'd be like number nineteen. You think you're gonna go on around eleven, but you end up going on about two in the morning. And you come back, and then finally, someone out there says, "Oh, you know what, you don't have to wait in line next week. You've got some good stuff. Come back and we'll put you on last." So after a few months of that, you're on at three in the morning, and you start working your way up.

Paul, the class is getting ready to go up on stage at a club soon, and many of them are nervous. After seeing that tape of your first shot on *The Tonight Show* with Johnny Carson, I thought it would be good for you to tell them how you dealt with nervousness on your first *Tonight Show* or your first time on stage.

The first time going up on stage in New York, it was sort of like Carson in that it was so exciting that the thrill of doing it overshadowed the fear. Especially doing Carson. If I'd thought about the reality of this going out to millions of people, I don't know what I could've done with that information. To me, it was exciting because it was a goal that I'd always had. So I kind of focused on that. I studied piano in college and my piano teacher said that when you're performing, your adrenaline will probably kick in and make you want to go faster, so slow down, and if you think you're going too slow, slow down even more. Because your gauge is off. What you think is happening isn't really happening because you're so charged.

How long had you been doing stand-up before your first shot on The Tonight Show?

I'd been doing stand-up like three years. And I don't know if I was ready to do Carson, but it was the week that *Diner* opened, so I went on, and the stuff was the best of whatever material I had at the time.

Did you see any other connection or similarity that you can take from studying music and apply to doing stand-up?

One thing that I want to share in terms of performance is just slowing it down, and I learned this more with stand-up. But I have noticed similarities in that I play piano the way I do comedy in that they all kinda form together. Like when I speak, I do run-on sentences and try not to fall into predictable patterns. And I realize that when I play I do that. If I'm playing a melody and you think you can hum it, well, I'm going to change it, because I don't want you to hum it. So if you think you know where I'm going with a joke, I'll go over here and do this joke. Which is why I have a very, very, small audience.

When I was starting out, I would throw out a routine no matter how funny it was if I saw that people would figure out where it was headed. It would bother me that someone could predict my mind.

I've seen that in a destructive way. I've seen some comedians come up with a bit in a club that makes a small audience or comedians in the back laugh, and then when it starts to become requested, they won't do it because they don't want to be on demand. It's not a particularly healthy thing for longevity. After all, Sinatra still sings "The Lady Is a Tramp."

Was there any comedian or comedians who inspired you to try stand-up?

Most people, myself included, watch comedians on TV and go, "I could do that." Watching a mediocre comic will trigger you. You're not inspired by greatness, you're inspired by mediocrity. Because if you saw somebody great, you go, Why even bother?

Was there a particular mediocre comedian?

I'll tell you later. No, actually, it wasn't that he was mediocre, it was a guy I knew in college. In my freshman year, I had done stand-up in clubs like once. And then one year, during the summer, I met this guy who was an emcee, and by the end of the school year, this guy was on Carson. And it wasn't that he was bad, but it allowed me to see the route. I said, "Wow, he was just doing nothing last July, and by going on stage, he had gotten a lot better by putting in the hours." It was like you do this, take the following steps, and you end up on television.

Who were your influences when you were starting?

Stylistically, Robert Klein was like a big one for almost everybody starting out.

More so than George Carlin?

Well, both. We used to go see Carlin and Klein in the village like twenty years ago. But Klein more for me, just because I felt that Carlin was less accessible to me. He was more like an out-there hippie guy. Woody Allen's albums. In fact, the first five minutes I ever did, when I listened to it, it sounded like really bad Woody

Allen—and I realized the absurdity of trying to be Woody Allen. Then sometimes I'd imitate David Brenner. He dressed really well, so I'd wear a suit. Then I said, "Wait a minute, you're seventeen, don't wear a suit. That's not you." So you really have to find your own style, and it takes a long time. There's really no shortcut, and you can't be impatient. I don't know what a person's goals are individually, but if it's something that they think they want to do for a long time, then the goals have to be set accordingly, which is why you can't be in a rush. If *The Tonight Show* people said, "Why don't you go on with Jay tomorrow?" you might be tempted to do it, but it would be foolish. Because you want to wait. The job will be there. Getting on *The Tonight Show* is the easiest job in the world because all they look for is good comics. If you're a good comic, there is no challenge, you'll be on. The hard thing is getting good enough to be there.

How important is individuality to you as a comedian?

That's really what style and writing and performing are about, finding your avenue. You go to a club and you see twenty people do bits about TV and relationships. Like, how many arenas are there? But what's important is where they go with it. Cosby does a wife joke, and Dangerfield does a wife joke and they're entirely different. They take you into their own world. It's where you go and how you take that scene that makes it stand out.

How do you write your material? Are you a pen-and-paper person or a tape-recorder person?

I'm still figuring that out. I kind of scribble down the ideas, the subject. I'll think there's something funny about this, and I'll try it out on stage. Sort of like testing the waters. And if they laugh, then I'll go work on it. So a lot of times, I tell the audience, "Come back in a month, this will be really funny, but tonight, it's just practice."

Say you try something out and they don't laugh, yet you still feel there's something funny there. What will you do?

I'll try it again. At certain points, you have to say, Okay, it's just me. Depends what style of comedy you're doing. If you're Steven Wright, who is his own bag, and you're doing something sort of absurdist, it doesn't have to ring true. It just has to be funny. If you're doing stuff that's personal, the category that I work in, then you say, Well, this is funny to me, I wonder if this is funny to you. So literally you just put it out there, and you find out that, oh boy, that really is just my family. I don't know if it was Cosby or somebody else who said years ago that very often the most personal will turn out to be the most universal. Because everybody does have a family and everybody does eat and talk about women. It depends on how you do it artistically. So when you hit something on the head, it's really rewarding for you and the audience. You'll hear people in the audience say, "That's my family, that's my life, that happened to me when I got my new car," or whatever it is. And a lot of times I feel rewarded, too, and I feel comforted by their laughs.

So you do a lot of writing on stage?

I've never been one to just sit down and write. For me, it's easier to write on stage, and then listen to the tapes at home, and go, Take that out, put this in. That for me is the fun part, the tweaking and trying to find a magic word that makes the whole bit come together.

Do you pull a lot of your material from when you're just sitting and talking with your friends.

Yeah. Half of the key to being a good comic is literally keeping a pad around. And knowing what to do with it. Very often it's just subjects. I mean, I have fragments, bits, and books full of stuff where there's something funny in there.

Have you ever had anybody write for you, or do you write everything on your own?

Lately I had people talk with me and give me ideas that I'll rewrite. Sometimes if I have a TV shot to do, I'll call friends and I'll go, "Is this funny?" And we'll jam, but very rarely can somebody just give me something and I'll go, It works.

Why wouldn't something work for you?

Because for me, I think of myself as a stand-up more than a writer. It kind of has to come out of my mouth, and even if I write down exactly what I said performing, I look at it and go, That's not funny. So if someone hands me a piece of paper, I'll try it and say it, and then I'll find a way to reword it that feels more natural to myself.

You can't say it in their words?

Right, yeah. But you eventually find your way.

Do you stick exactly to the words on paper, or do you allow yourself to be creative when you perform?

I allow myself the freedom, but ultimately you may find something that works, and you find, boy, it's these words that are funny. I allow myself the freedom until I find that. And then sometimes you do the joke and it works, and then three months later it's not working.

Have you every caught yourself doing old material with a kind of recitative delivery?

Sometimes.

How do you bring yourself out of that and say something old in a fresh way?

Sometimes I'll reshuffle the order and it'll give a different approach to the subject. You may discover a new way to get into it. Sometimes you just put it away. It's like a shirt that you've worn a little too much. Sometimes you outgrow things. What was always so exemplary and great about Cosby is that if you look at his work for the last thirty years, he grew up with it: his parents, grandparents, his childhood friends, his wife, his young kids, his college kids, his kids moving out. Not only is that his style, but he never has to turn outside his life for material, and it just came from an honest place. It's where he's coming from. Which is what you should all be doing—saying, "Here's where I'm coming from."

Did the idea for *Mad About You* come from your monologue about being newly married?

Yes. I was doing a lot of stand-up and the stuff that was working and I was really enjoying doing, was the stuff that I was doing about, relationships, about marriage. For me because it was true, I had to be a little courageous and thought, Maybe I shouldn't share this stuff. And then I got rewarded. So when I was coming up with the idea for the show, I thought that I really wanted to do that arena, really bring it very personal. I wanted to create a show where I wouldn't have to stretch the character to force the material in. I said, This stuff's funny when I say it to my friends, this stuff's funny on stage. How do I keep that and make a show that is real and similar to the situation? What makes it easier is that instead of having to create the arena like in stand-up where you say, "I'm home with my wife, and she brings something home," you paint a picture. In the show you have the apartment, you have the wife walking in the door with whatever it is you're talking about, and you just say exactly what you said in the routine.

Sounds like a pretty smooth transition.

Yeah, a different approach to getting the same material out.

How does it feel compared to doing your stand-up since now you're getting your laughs from the same material that you used in stand-up?

It's weird. I don't really like the laugh I get from the audience. The performer in me does, but it's distracting.

Why?

Because when we're working the show, we're creating a real living room, bedroom and it feels very intimate. So the laughter is jolting.

Does it throw your timing off?

It throws the timing off, for one, and it also sort of taps that performer in me, so if they laugh when you give a little raised eyebrow, you go for five raised eyebrows, which is not what people do. It's like I love it, but I don't want it. So don't put people there laughing, because I'm going to chase them. I'm going to start doing stand-up.

You've done small clubs, concerts in larger venues, and television. How do you adapt to the different arenas?

One piece of advice given to me early on was to just put the room where you are most comfortable into your head.

Can you give an example?

Like I know how to do the Catch a Rising Star club at two in the morning, but I don't know how to do this theater, so when I'm at the theater I pretend it's two in the morning at Catch a Rising Star. I know where I feel comfortable, and I know I feel funnier around certain people than others. So I get into the mindset, "Okay, where do I feel comfortable? I feel funny with these people in this situation and these circumstances." So put yourself there and that will bring you out in your best light. But there is really no advice short of learning by doing it, getting up there in different situations and finding what works and what doesn't. That and a really good hat.

CHRIS ROCK
"I Feel I'm Using All I Have"

Chris Rock is a stand-up comedian with a searingly honest point of view, one that forces people to laugh as they confront the truth. His 1996 HBO special *Bring the Pain* (filled with intensity, energy, and bitingly funny social commentary) was thought-provoking stand-up comedy at its best. Dressed in black and prowling the stage like a gospel-preaching panther, he had people comparing him to Richard Pryor. Listening to the intelligent, informed content of Chris's act, you'd never guess that he's an eleventh-grade dropout. A voracious reader of newspapers, he possesses an inquisitive, skeptical mind of all he surveys. Selling out concerts all over the country, host of his own show on HBO, with a new comedy CD out, a well-received book of his daring comic musings, commercials running on national TV, a role in the film *Lethal Weapon 4*, and three Emmy awards, Chris Rock has established himself as a ubiquitous presence and a strong, original force in the world of comedy.

I was witness to Chris's burgeoning popularity and ascension to the next level up close in 1996. I was writing with Chris and another stand-up-comedian-turned-writer/producer named Jeff Stilson for *Politically Incorrect*'s political convention coverage. We were working on Chris's daily five-minute segments. Whenever we went out with Chris in public, he was recognized and approached by hordes of people of all ages and races. Even policemen were having their pictures taken with him. It got pretty overwhelming for him sometimes, and one night he decided not to go to a party 'cause he didn't want to deal with all the people who would be coming up to him. So I asked him, If he could make the same amount of money he's making now doing a job behind the scenes so that he wouldn't have to be swarmed in public, would he do that? "That's a good question," he said. "Let me think about that." He thought about it for a moment and then said, "No. Because I have to perform."

Every night when we would finish shooting his segment for *Politically Incorrect*, Chris would jump in car and go find a comedy club to work out in. He couldn't get enough of it. It was stark evidence that, despite his many creative and lucrative activities and opportunities, his most intense focus is still first and foremost on striving for excellence with his stand-up comedy. This interview was conducted at Duke's restaurant on Sunset Boulevard on May 23, 1997.

CHRIS ROCK

I noticed as we came in here that you grabbed three newspapers, and I remember you telling me that you used to read newspapers as a kid.

I gotta have a newspaper in front of me to even eat a meal.

Is reading newspapers a vital part of your development of material?

I guess on some level it is. To know the pulse of everything around you helps, but what I found out helps me the most with getting material is just being quiet around a lot of people. Like at functions, say somebody dies and the family is around, I just be quiet and take it all in. Take it all in. Just be a big sponge and listen to people who you want to ignore. Really listen to them, because they're going to say some little thing you can use. They can't help it.

Are you in an obsessive mode now about your stand-up comedy show?

Yeah, I'm very obsessive.

What form does that obsession take?

I'm just overly conscious of not wanting to be bad or mediocre. I want to be spent when the show is over. I want it to feel like I've just had good sex where there's nothing you can do afterwards.

Are we talking physically, mentally—

Physically and mentally. My throat hurts when the show is over, I can't think when it's over. Not that I can't think, but I don't want to think when it's over.

Why is your mind so tired after you do your show?

Because even though I know the jokes, I'm still looking for that ad-lib. I'm wondering, Is it there, is it here? I'm constantly feeling the audience.

On some nights when your mind is working hard searching for that new material or line, do you experience frustration on the nights when there isn't anything new there?

No, not really. The only frustration at this point is if something goes wrong technically like with the sound system, but right now I've really got my show down.

How much does your show fluctuate or change on a nightly basis?

Fifteen, twenty minutes at the most.

Do you ever change the order of your show?

Yeah, I'll change the order sometimes.

Can you start your show at any point?

I could do it, 'cause I have the experience and the savvy to do it, but I look at my jokes like a team. Some guys are lead-off hitters, some guys are clean-up hitters. The stuff I do at the end really belongs at the end. My first joke is really just a joke, a basic joke that Henny Youngman could tell, but I don't do that type of joke at the end. The thing at the end should encompass the whole show.

When did you develop the concept of putting your show together that way?

It really came naturally. Watching Pryor, watching Eddie Murphy in *Delirious*, I saw that everything tied up at the end like a movie. I'm in concert now, and there's definitely a jump from clubs to doing concerts. A concert is like a movie, like a play. It really should all tie together. It really should be a show, not just a collection of jokes.

Do you work on your act primarily on stage or off stage when you're on the road?

Primarily on stage. Usually before I got out on the road I work out in clubs, piecing my show together. Another thing I do when I go out on the road is take a friend who has his own career to open the show for me. It helps keep up that camaraderie that you used to have when you worked clubs, and would go to the diner together afterward and go over your acts. This way, after a show, you can't help but talk about your show. I talk about his show, he talks about mine. Like two baseball players.

You've been on a roll since your HBO special *Bring the Pain* and you're in non-stop demand. Are you in control of your career, or is your career in control of you?

Right now my career is a good career because my career is caused by the people. I'm not someone who's been created by this town here, Hollywood. I've got a core audience who's willing to pay to see me in any market.

Tell me a little about your pre-show ritual if you have one. At what time do you start getting ready for your concert?

It's not really about what I do before the show, it's about what I don't do.

What is it that you don't do?

I like to really do nothing and be around as few people as possible. I look at the whole day as the show—as a day of work.

Do you walk on stage with adrenaline pumping each time, or are you feeling neutral?

It's weird. It's different every night because I change every day. Some nights I'm depressed, but as soon as they introduce me, it's all gone. I hear the music, and the people getting into it, and I know that as soon as I step out there, there's going to be a roar, so whatever down feelings I had are all gone.

How does doing bigger venues change your performance? Do you have to be bigger physically?

I do more physical stuff. I walk back and forth to use the whole stage, and I'm more alert because I'm trying to fill up the whole room. I don't miss the clubs at all. I still use them to work out but I hope I never have to work a club again.

You once said in an interview that sometimes a comedian just has to ask the right question, and often that is the essence of the humor.

Just an elementary question that seems obvious once it's stated. They're not really jokes in the classic sense.

Are you taping your shows?

Every show with an audio cassette.

Do you listen to them every night?

Not every night—only if I did something different will I listen to it. But I keep them all, and I'll listen to all of them before I start my next show.

Is it fun listening to them or tedious?

It's tedious, very tedious. But you've gotta do it.

Would you say that you trust your comedic instincts now?

Oh, totally?

Do you trust them as much when you're sitting down writing your book as you do when you're doing your stand-up?

I trust them even more then. When you're on stage doing stand-up, you're competing with the greats of all time. Writing a humorous book, I'm competing with Terry McMillan. The bar's a little lower.

But now a lot of comedians are doing books: Carlin, Cosby, Seinfeld, Reiser, Sinbad.

Yeah, but I'm competing with them in a medium that they're not even strong in. I mean, none of us is really strong in it.

Woody Allen?

Woody Allen is the one. My book is like his style-wise. Thirty percent is my material, but the rest is just weird, imaginative stuff.

Do you like writing that kind of stuff?

I love it. I used to like it even when I was a kid.

Does some of that find its way into your stand-up?

Oh yeah. You can slip the absurd into a normal joke. For example I used to do a joke about no one wants to be an organ donor. Then I'd slip in, "What if you come back from the dead and now you have no eyes?"

Why did you title your HBO special *Bring the Pain*?

It was a line from the rap record "Method Man" by the Wu-Tang Clan. The line was, "I've come to bring the pain, hardcore to your brain," and it got me hyped. I said to myself, That's strong—this guy means business.

Did you come up with this title before or after you did the special?

I came up with the title after the special 'cause I saw that his attitude fit my attitude. I felt that it was time for me to make a statement.

One of the things that I noticed was a preacher-like element in your delivery. Is there a lot of church in your background?

My grandfather's a reverend, and when I started doing comedy along with my comedy albums, I bought the albums of orators like Dr. King, Malcolm X, and JFK just to listen to them talk, and see how they commanded audiences, because I felt that even if you don't think it's funny, I don't want you to think it's boring.

Explain the statement, "The material takes you as far as it can take you."

I'd see guys getting mad 'cause their career wasn't moving, and I'd say, "Well write some new jokes." Every new batch of jokes took me where it was gonna take me. When I stopped writing, the career stayed right there.

Where is your starting place for a joke?

The main thing for me is the topic. What do I want to talk about? For example, if you're with a woman and you don't get married, every minute a woman spends with a man she didn't marry she considers wasted time. Meanwhile, you could've traveled the world together and had a great time. I'm trying to figure out how I really feel about it in a comedic way.

You're working a lot and you're by your own admission in top form comedically. How does it feel?

I feel I'm using all I have. I actually hope I'm not at the top of my game since I'm only thirty-two.

When were you aware that you had taken your comedy to another level?

When I got to the point where I wasn't really competing with other comedians. I used to look at Damon Wayans and Tommy Davidson, guys who really acted stuff out, and I used to think I wasn't a good performer because I didn't do that. Once I got over that, I was all right.

What got you over that?

I just got more confident.

Are you striving for greatness or excellence in your stand-up?

I would say I'm striving for excellence, but in the overall picture, I'm definitely striving for greatness.

Where do you see the room for improvement in your stand-up?

I could get more theatrical. I could really learn how to act things out—not become an impressionist per se, but really commit to a voice from time to time. Incorporate more quiet moments into the show. To me, that's the best part of the show, to bring them down and then *pow*, hit them with an explosive line. My physicality could get better. I use a lot of energy, but I'm still not really a good physical comedian by any stretch of the imagination. I could broaden my topics and really get into talking about emotions. I've definitely got a long way to go.

ROSEANNE

"I Want To Say Something That Has Some Sort Of Impact . . ."

Lucille Ball, Mary Tyler Moore, Roseanne: The three most powerful and influential women in television history. Through their television shows and personas, these three lady giants of the American television apocalypse have each defined a decade of our culture's media perceptions of women and wives. Lucy, Mary, and Roseanne. Ditzy, Vulnerable, and Earthy.

Once called "a Richard Pryor for women," Roseanne has fearlessly and defiantly challenged American convention at every turn. An iconoclast of the first order, armed with insight and bite, Roseanne's staunch and relentless belief in her point of view on marriage, men, and family life enabled her to turn a family sitcom into something truly groundbreaking and revelatory. Much like the woman herself.

When I finally got in touch with Roseanne, she was in the midst of a lot of transitional activity, both personal and professional. She was in a thoughtful mood as we conducted this interview by phone on August 1, 1997.

ROSEANNE

In watching your HBO special *Domestic Goddess,* I was struck by the similar way you and the late, great Sam Kinison both raise and lower your voices in your delivery, and the raw emotionalism you express at times. Are you and Sam kindred spirits in comedy?

I first met Sam years ago in Colorado when he came there to perform, and I was opening for him and we both admired each other's comedy. We both had a lot in common and we talked about it frequently. Sam had been a child preacher, and so had I and we both used what we had learned from that in our stand-up deliveries.

That's interesting because Chris Rock told me that he had studied the great orators to help him with his delivery. In your special, there is a bit of a preaching tone about the indignities of being a housewife.

The use of language and the rise and fall of tone in my delivery and the control of the stage is what I learned from being a preacher.

I noticed in some of your speech patterns and inflections a similarity to black speech patterns, like you would start a sentence and end it with "and shit." Is there a black influence on your comedy?

Richard Pryor was a huge influence on me. Plus, I've always had a lot of black friends. We were working-class people and I worked in a bookstore with a lot of black people and people like me, and I guess I saw a huge influence there. And I loved Dick Gregory so much. He was just awesome to me. I still see him occasionally and talk to him. I love what he did. He told me that at some point it wasn't just about being funny anymore, which I admired because I feel that way.

You must've had an interest in comedy for a long time.

Since I was three years old. I watched *Ed Sullivan* every Sunday. All I lived for was the comedians. I knew that was somewhere I would go. To me they were like prophets. I still have that kind of respect for all comics.

In watching your riffs on marriage, I realized that Phyllis Diller was kind of like a precursor to you with her flamboyant outrageousness and cackling laugh.

She definitely paved the way for me. But I think Mae West paved the way for every single comic, even Lenny Bruce, the way she controlled her material and flew in the face of every convention. Watching her made me think I could do this because the way I perceived her was that she was inside the stereotype and destroying it from the middle. I knew I could do that as a woman because I always saw so much in my family about women and men that I thought was ridiculous.

One of the things I noticed is that you're a Scorpio and that many gender barriers have been broken down by Scorpio women like Billie Jean King in tennis and Katherine Hepburn, who stated that she lived her life like a man. Were you aware of that?

It may be a Scorpio thing because Scorpio karma has such a strong spiritual yearning, and strong physical desires and that the Scorpio goal is to get those things to not be at war. I think it's why Scorpio women dare to do things that other women don't because we go so high.

I've dealt with some Scorpio women in my life, and I am now on a Scorpio woman sabbatical. I'm a Taurus and Scorpio is my polar opposite. It's an interesting mix, but there's a lot of conflict.

My first husband was a Taurus and there was a lot of conflict.

Tell me a little about your early writing methods. Was there a disciplined process?

How I'd write stuff was that I would think about it for about six years and then it would come out in one day. People would be surprised about how much it was developed, but I'd thought about it for a long time. I think I was formulating my act from the time that I was little watching TV. So that everything that happened to me, I would think, "Well, this'll fit into my act." 'Cause I knew I was gonna do it.

Did you have notebooks or journals?

I've got hundreds of notebooks, journals, cocktail napkins, toilet paper, anything that I could find to write on. First I'd start off with this great theoretical premise, or poetry about that 1960's injustice kind of shit, and then I would boil it down to where I could say it in a sentence, and from there it would become jokes. It's so much about language.

I noticed that you would sometimes use an eloquent phrase like "particularly festive," which would present a striking contrast coming from a gum-chewing, wise-cracking, working-class woman.

I got a lot of that from W.C. Fields, who I just loved. I stole timing off him. He was saying pretty eloquent things filtered through class as well.

There's an emotional content in your material in that it seems to be coming from your soul, not just your head.

It's just trying to put everything in its place. I think that's what we comedians try to do—to organize the world according to what we feel is right.

One of the things about your stage presence is the subtext, "I don't give a fuck." You're going to say what you want to say and let the chips fall.

That's what it's about, isn't it?

Did you have that attitude from Jump Street?

Yes. In fact, I always thought the funny thing about me was that I didn't give a shit.

That's obvious in the way you deliver a provocative line and just stand there and let it soak in with the audience.

Yes. You hit them with it. If you look at the language of comedy, it's kinda like a violent attack on their consciousness in a way. I think we want to hit people in the head, so their head will open up. We know that people don't buy the crazy shit in the world because we don't.

What do you think makes for a strong stand-up stage presence?

I think that it's a calling from a higher consciousness that shows through to the audience when they see your commitment to what you're saying.

Do you see that in the new comedians?

No, because they don't seem to be doing it for the reasons that we did it. They're doing it only for material reasons. What the fuck are they talking about? They're not saying anything.

Would you say that your comedy is fueled by anger and frustration?

People on a low level spiritually see it as anger, but people on a higher level see it as indignation with a moral weight to it. That's why it's so hard to talk about it, because unless someone is right where you are, it's hard to communicate. We're the people who say it for people who can't say it. With respect to comedy, I don't find it funny to make fun of how people look. I don't think it's funny to make fun of people who are different than me. I think the fun stuff is to make fun of the way we all think.

It seems that you were influenced by the social-commentary spirit that came out of the late sixties, early seventies.

It was a time when the world really did change and I was affected by it. Because the world really did change in our generation, and now it's changing back. It seems that the proverbial intolerance is back.

What do you think has caused that?

I think that there's a materialism that's totally out of control. I think that people have spiritual hunger, but they're trying to fill it up with material things. That's the battle that people of consciousness and people of conscience have—to come forward and try to change things back to something more positive. Like heaven and hell, and good and evil, that battle is always here.

Do you have any urge to do stand-up anymore?

I went to the Montreal Comedy Festival and did a little stand-up. I was taking questions from the audience and talking to people, being funny that way. I don't write material anymore because I like the jamming and jazz aspect of it now. I guess after doing it for ten, fifteen years, you can start jamming live, which is what I like now, because the rest of it seems like a little school-girl recitation.

It's interesting that you use jamming, a musical term, to describe comedy.

I've always thought that comedy was about music and jazz. And also math with its numbers and balancing timing.

Out of material, delivery, point of view, and timing, what's the most important?

All of it. It's to be able to orchestrate your act so that they're all balanced, and one doesn't drown out the other. You have to make sure that all the parts blend.

What was your strongest part?

Because I was like the first woman to really break the shit down, I had to have all of them, but I'm really proud of my writing. I think my timing was great, and the way I used my voice was great. I used to think of it like a clarinet. I worked really hard to hear the music in my comedy. Sometimes when I couldn't hear the music, then I'd know I was no good. I knew I wasn't ready because it didn't sound like music. When I could hear the music, that's when I left for L.A. I knew I was ready.

What do you really get out of being on stage?

I like the free speech part of it. I want to say something that has some sort of impact, and then have it be funny as well. I wouldn't walk across the street just to be funny. Awhile back, I went to a club in Pasadena to do some stand-up and when I had finished this killer joke, all people wanted to know was if John Goodman was easy to work with, etcetera. They wanted to see me as only Roseanne Conner, a kinda not-dangerous woman, not the comic me. I mean, Roseanne Conner has a little bit of my stand-up in her, but my stand-up is different from her. My stand-up is dangerous, and she's dangerous too in a more comfortable way. That made me back up from doing stand-up for quite a while.

Tell me a little bit about the clash between the stand-up sensibility and the sitcom sensibility when you moved to network television.

My biggest battles came about because I was a woman, and it was my stand-up, and I was saying something about being a woman in stand-up, and a million other mirrors. That's what made it hard for me. The traditional sitcom writers couldn't even conceive of that. It was like I was a stranger from a strange land. To me there was no woman's voice or woman's humor in it. I'd go to people and say what I'd want and they couldn't write it. It's even more insidious than that. It's like their sexism couldn't be separated from the material. I was into the message and controlling the message, because everything has a message whether you think it does or doesn't. It does. And I just won't la-de-da for anybody. I didn't come here to be your fat, favorite aunt.

You hired mostly stand-up comedians to write for your show when you assumed control. Why?

I thought they had less preconceived notions and formulas and because I think that stand-ups are braver than writers. I expected my writers to think, I expected my writers to write, and I expected them to fix it if I didn't like it. But there are very few people who have that kind of talent. And the unfortunate thing is that they usually have their own deals, and they don't need me.

JERRY SEINFELD

"It's Just Getting Your Ass From Upright To Seated"

Clarity. That's what I think of when I think of Jerry Seinfeld. Stripped down. Simple. Zen in approach. A supremely confident yet modest man, he's created a funny, farcical, financial phenomena in American television history with his classic situation comedy *Seinfeld*, and Jerry views all the attendant hoopla with detached bemusement. His routines and subsequent show reveal that he is a master of the minutiae of daily life—a steady accretion of numerous small details until the inevitable meaning and laughs well up and erupt. Genially aloof, he's the "Asian-Jewish Man," as he's referred to himself to me on several occasions.

Of all the comedians I've known, I've always found Jerry to be the most disciplined in his writing and working habits. Yet without the accompanying stress or "whiffs" of angst-driven compulsion. A few years ago I was at The Improv in Los Angeles working out some material for a *Tonight Show* appearance the next night, and I happened to mention to Jerry that I hadn't been on a stage in a month. Jerry, who at that time was working over three hundred days a year doing stand-up, was astonished. "You're the anti-me," he said.

While everybody cannot be as single-minded and disciplined as Jerry, his analytical and concise revelation of his writing methods will give any beginning comedian a bedrock foundation from which to begin their own adventures into creating and developing comedic material. The interview was given at my class in the summer of 1992.

JERRY SEINFELD

Describe your method of getting into writing a routine.

I believe in having a structured approach. My philosophy is that I can sit down at any time with a problem, and if I sit there and don't allow my mind to have distractions—no phone, no music, no television—my mind will eventually start to work on it on its own. It's like a biosphere situation. I isolate myself—'cause this is my "sit" time.

How long do you try to write or sit?

I say, "I'm going to sit for an hour." I always consider sitting the accomplishment. If I could boil it down to the essence of becoming a really fine comedian, it's just getting your ass from upright to seated.

Was this your approach when you first started developing material?

This was my approach from the very beginning. At first I'd just go on stage and try this and try that, but I soon felt that I had to have a better system than that if I was going to survive the talk shows. I had to figure out how I was going to create material on a dependable basis. That is the number one problem that a comedian has to confront in the early years, so that when the time comes that the demand is put on you to appear on a show like

The Tonight Show three or four times a year, you can come up with the material.

So your first sit-down goal was an hour a day?

Yes. An hour a day. That was my first goal. Ten hours a month. That's not easy for someone starting out, and it took me a couple of years to accomplish. Sometimes I had to trick myself to get myself to write. You wouldn't believe the things I had to do to get myself to write. Sometimes I'd put the cookies by my notebook. It's like a mousetrap—I go get the cookies, then I look in the notebook, and the next thing I know, I'm writing.

How do you pick a subject to write about?

That's just an instinct. Frankly, I think you've gotta be born with that. I look at something and go, "That's weird, there's something funny about it. I don't know what it is, but I betcha if I think about it, I can figure it out."

What was the subject matter of the first routine you wrote?

It was about being left-handed—about how everything in society is set up against us. It was about discrimination. (Laughing) So you can see that even at the beginning, it was very political. By the way, most comedians are left-handed. Way more than the general population.

Did you get laughs relatively soon when you started out?

Yeah, pretty early. I was lucky in that people understood what I was talking about and they seemed to know who I was as a person. That's a big thing in comedy. If people can get a quick sense of who you are, they relax. The worst I did was bomb every other show—which was tolerable.

How can a beginning comedian avoid bombing?

You can't avoid it when you're starting because you just don't know what's going on. For example,s you don't have the experience to know that you're talking too fast or that you're talking in a rote fashion instead of in the present moment.

Did you tape your shows?

Yes I did, and I still do.

What did you look for when you listened to your tapes?

In those days it was just pure survival. Anything that got a laugh I would do. Even if it was something that I probably shouldn't have been doing. People think of comedians as people who are outgoing and comfortable in front of people, when in fact it's just the opposite. What you are trying to become skilled at is "embarrassment avoidance."

What kept you going when you were bad in the beginning?

It wasn't fame, it wasn't money, and it still isn't. I was in love with the process of putting together a joke.

Who were some of your early influences?

You were one of my influences. You had that comedy album with the Ajax can on it. Robert Klein. But Bill Cosby was the first comedian I became obsessed with when I was young—listening to his album *Why Is There Air?* I was entranced by him. I had every album, and I memorized every routine. That's why I see Bill Cosby as a hero. He was the first comedian to make me laugh. As a matter of fact, his skill was what first made me realize how wonderful it could be to make people laugh.

Should people imitate their influences?

It's pretty hard to avoid when you're just starting, but if you stay with it long enough, that will fall away and you will emerge out of it. That's the goal—to become yourself.

How long did it take you to figure out your individual comedic essence?

I'd say ten years. It's always changing because as human being you're always changing. There's always other things that you want to talk about, and feel you're able to talk about, but I don't believe in searching for it. That leads to hooks and personas instead of human beings and three-dimensional people on stage, which I believe an audience enjoys seeing more than anything else. So I would say a person should write everything that they think about, and they'll naturally enjoy talking about a percentage of those things. Then they'll naturally start to edit out those things they don't feel comfortable about. But that takes time.

How would you describe the point of view of your material?

My material is reality with a personal twist. I try to come up with things that almost make too much sense.

Do you write much material on stage when you work?

Yes, there's kind of a gear that you kick into. This started happening more when I started doing forty-five minutes and up. I started to relax and ad-lib off routines that I'd already worked out. All of my longer routines have developed that way.

Now that you have a television show, is it difficult having to say words that you haven't written for yourself?

I work with writers on the stand-up segment, and also on the dialogue, and I'll hear a line and I'll go, "No, I can't do that line, that's not me." I know myself well enough to know when I don't feel comfortable with a line.

Now that your television show is popular, when you are giving a concert, how do you deal with the adulation that may have to do more with your show than your stand-up routine?

Some of the audiences are bubbly. They start screaming out character names and plots from the show, and it's a little intrusive. I try to
be gracious about it. You have to approach them in the same way
you approach a big audience, which is, I'm here to do this and I'm
gonna do it. That has to be subconsciously felt by the audience. You
have to take control. They have to feel your intention. Bill Cosby once
told me, "When you're the pilot of the plane, you can't come on the
P.A. system and go, 'Well, I'm gonna try and take her up.'"

**Your disciplined approach seems to illustrate that a person needs
more than just a good sense of humor to succeed as a stand-up
comedian.**

Being funny is part of it, but not all of what it takes to be a successful comedian. To figure out an audience is the work of becoming a
comedian. Once figured out, that's when it becomes fun.

**In the final analysis, what do you get out of being a stand-up
comedian?**

It's fun to be funny. It's great to be funny. It's as much fun to be
funny as it is to have someone be funny for you. Being on either
side of that equation is just the most wonderful thing in life.

GARRY SHANDLING
"Why Isn't It Enough To Be Funny"

Garry Shandling is a gentle, funny, and complicated man. The creator and star of Showtime's *It's Garry Shandling's Show,* and HBO's *Larry Sanders,* two highly acclaimed and innovative comedy shows, Garry is also one of the cleverest stand-ups to have come down the pike. Building a stage act filled with an angst second only to Richard Lewis, Garry always had a subtle unpredictability to his punchlines, followed by sardonically casual afterthought lines. In 1979, I played a week at the San Diego Improv with Garry and got to watch his show every night. I found it interesting that he changed both the order and the substance of his show every night. Though his persona is one of neurosis and fearfulness, in his stage work and in his television shows he always fearlessly puts forth the subtle truth of things as he sees them. This interview was conducted at his office in Studio City on July 11, 1996.

GARRY SHANDLING

I recently watched your two cable stand-up specials, *Alone in Vegas*, and *Stand-Up*, and I noticed a shift in the pace of your delivery in that you moved from a faster pace to a slower—

More conversational pace.

Right.

That was the intent. When I first started doing stand-up, I did all jokes. I wrote what I call hard jokes. Like my sex life, which is somewhat less than—

A hard joke.

Right. So my struggle was always to be more conversational, and in fact if I do another stand-up special, which I hope to do in the next couple of years, it will be even more conversational. So it's like cutting more of that joke fat off.

Yet, back in 1979 when we worked The Improv together in San Diego, I felt you had a conversational style of delivery even then.

I'm sure that it was always my inclination, but like any comic, I veer off of it out of fear occasionally and just go for the joke. So I think the struggle is to somehow find the line between being funny and conversational, without being indulgent.

I noticed that you did more long stories in your Garry Shandling *Stand-Up* special.

I get credit for doing long stories, but the truth is, I did long stories because I didn't have enough life experience to draw on for material because I was spending so much time doing *Larry Sanders*. So I took one story and milked it for all it was worth.

You've hit on an interesting point. Now that my life has kind of settled down, and I'm not having crazy love affairs, I wonder where my material is going to come from now.

It's funny, because we're writing an episode of the show in which the head writer isn't writing any funny jokes for Larry, and then breaks up with his girlfriend, and he starts writing really funny jokes. And he's actually afraid to get back into a happy relationship because he's afraid he won't be funny anymore. Because so much of humor comes from pain. So, unfortunately, I still tune into my pain and write funny stuff because I can tune into my pain. But I think it's a struggle as you get older and grow to continue to reinvent and find new places to go with that pain and discuss and find new topics. That's why I admire George Carlin, because he seems to continue to find the things that sort of honestly bother him, and talk about them on stage.

But you come out of your personal life, and George never—

George is a little more objective. I'm a little more subjective, so everything has to come really out of my own personal pain. And George is angrier than I am at society.

That's the same with Bill Maher and Dennis Miller: They're coming from a societal look, so the newspaper can always help create their material.

I attempt at times to look at it, and I care about society and those things on a large scale, but I find it naturally more difficult for me to write about than my own personal struggles.

Which brings me to an interesting thing I observed when watching your last special—it seemed to be angst-free and rather upbeat.

I'm sure in my next one I'll be beating myself up again. But you're right. I challenged myself not to go back to the self-deprecating humor that worked in the past because I think we can all get into a rut that is ultimately destructive. Plus, I don't feel as self-deprecating in real life as I did ten years ago. I feel good enough about myself that I can make fun of others now. Are these sunglasses bothering you by the way?

No, they just make you look cooler than I've ever thought of you before.

I'm cooler than you thought I am. I'm cooler than people think I am. See, there's no self-deprecating.

Do you remember when your style of delivery changed?

Yes. In 1984. I had a bad break-up with a woman. It was like a very short relationship, but I was hurt, because it was in the infatuation stage, and she dumped me. And I was in a comedy club in Dallas, and I went up on stage, and I said, "I just broke up with my girlfriend because she moved in with another guy." And I started talking about relationships and how difficult they were, which was the first time I didn't do just jokes. And later when I was ready to do another *Tonight Show*, Jim McCawley (talent coordinator at that time) came to see me to see what I would do on the show, and he said to me, "You've really changed. The material is really conversational, and different, and not quite as funny, but let's try it." And it worked great and it was the beginning of my getting into the conversational delivery and being willing to talk about my pain even more than I had done prior to that.

Was that just following an impulse?

It was a complete impulse. I could hardly avoid it because I was in such pain, so I just walked up on stage and said, "Is there a shrink in the audience?" and just started talking as though the audience was a shrink. But I remember it as being a benchmark in my style.

So you didn't even care about whether you were going to get laughs or not?

Yeah, the event of breaking up with the woman was bigger than the event of being on stage. She said, "I want to start seeing other people". She didn't say men. It was like she might as well have said, "I want to start dating other mammals." It was like the broadest category she could find, and that's what I was talking about because that's what she said.

Was it cathartic for you do your stuff on stage? Did it get you through it?

Yeah, I think it's incredibly cathartic for me. I think it still helps me find who I am. I've honestly had my therapist say to me, "The same way you are on stage, you should be able to deal with your life like that." Which is, if you have somebody heckle you, you don't just stop and complain, you just take care of it. And he said that's how you have to live your life. So I think it's not unusual for actors or comedians to use the stage as a way of feeling free and good about their lives and in the moment. It's an interesting experience. Am I making any sense?

You're making a lot of sense.

In fact, I think that going in front of an audience is so cathartic for me that it's awkward for me to just go one-on-one with the shrink.

Do you still go to a shrink?

By a shrink, do you mean a psychologist? Or a psychiatrist? Or a psychotherapist?

What's the difference?

The answer's yes to all of them. I'll go see anybody who knows how to help me.

Do you think that comedians are more depressed than the average person in this society?

No, I think the average person probably is in pain in life, but they cover it, so you don't know they're depressed. Artists who are expressing their pain at least are not in denial.

Let's go back to how you started. You started as a writer initially, right?

Yeah, I moved to L.A. from Arizona to be a writer, not a performer. I wrote on *Sanford and Son* and *Welcome Back, Kotter.*

Were you on staff or freelancing?

I was freelancing both of those. Then I went on staff on the *Harvey Korman Show*, which was like one of those nine-episode short orders that never got picked up. Then I wrote pilots. And that's when I said, "I really don't want to do this anymore, I got to do stand-up." Because at least then I could do whatever I wanted. So if I failed, at least I knew *I* was failing.

Who were some of your influences when you were starting?

Woody Allen is my biggest influence. He had that pain that interested me. Pryor had a conversational style that really interested me, and I thought Carlin was genuinely funny back in the mid sixties when he was just starting.

Even before he grew his hair?

Yeah, once he grew the hair, I was a bigger fan.

That's when comedy became more anti-establishment, which was a sea change, wasn't it?

Yeah, he really reinvented himself. I think he's one of the really great stand-ups, like Lenny Bruce. He just continues to create new material. What's good about George is that in a really good way, he just doesn't care anymore about what others think of him. So he's free on stage to say what he thinks and believes.

Did you ever reach that stage?

No, I'm still too self-conscious. I think you can only be on stage what you are in life.

Were there any other artistic influences on your comedy?

That's a really good question.

The reason I asked is because in 1971 when I started out Carlin, Pryor, and Klein were anti-establishment and folksingers were anti-establishment and to me they seemed to be pursuing penetrating truths. And I said to myself, I would like to try to see if I could put that in my comedy.

I'll tell you the truth: I really think that's where I'm headed. I'm still evolving. I sense that I'm really having inner struggles going on with my artistic voice and what I want to say. I started out just going on stage sort of to be funny in whatever way that I'm funny, and to see if I could do it, and I really had to learn how to perform on stage. I had no idea. And I had to learn all of that, so now that I understand what it means to be on stage, now I have to look at what I really want to say. So I think that my art is really ahead of me. What is frustrating to me with any of my previous work is that I don't see the art in it. So there's very little of my work that I'm proud of. There are episodes of *Larry Sanders* that I think approach more of my artistic voice. So when I go back to stand-up, I want to make sure that I'm true to my artistic voice, whatever that appears to be.

You don't feel you've discovered it yet?

I don't think I've quite discovered it yet, but that may well be that's how all artists feel.

I used to hate my early albums, but then over the years, I learned to respect them more because people kept coming up to me and quoting from my albums and I could see how they stayed in people's minds. That made me lighten up on myself.

Yeah, but I think that your early stuff was artistic because it was very connected to your point of view, at least. I don't think my early stuff was artistic.

Did you bomb much when you first started?

For the first five years.

Are you serious? How did you hang in?

I thought that was part of how I grew as a person, being able to survive that. I think it made me a stronger person, and that was partly why I did it—to be able to survive that kind of brutality of going up on stage and being rejected.

Where did you start?

The first time I got on stage was in 1975, on an average night at The Comedy Store, and I did well. But I bombed every time thereafter for about fifteen times in a row on amateur night, until I stopped, and that's when I started writing television. Then two or three years later, after writing for television, I went back, did well the first time, and then started bombing again. And I was so frustrated that I said, I've got to figure this out. Then I devoted myself to it.

Were you taping yourself?

Yeah, I would always tape myself and listen. So I still feel any time I walk on stage that I could bomb, and absolutely, positively embarrass myself. I feel that every time I go on stage that that could happen. Now, I'm more willing to allow that to happen because I think you have to not give a shit in the best possible sense.

I had a clarinet teacher who used to say, "You can't get good if you can't take the punishment."

Yeah, I think you really have to be willing to bomb, and to fail, before you can be really good. If you're afraid to fail, you'll be bad. If you see an artist who's really afraid to fail, it's not someone you're going to like, and it's not someone who is doing real art. What they're really doing is looking for approval. I'll tell you something interesting if this means anything: I've met several professional athletes, and I'm always intimidated.

Why?

I've been trying to figure out why. One thing certainly is that my own athletic ability is less than what I wish it was. I play basketball, I'm your average white guy, and I can't dunk a donut into a cup of coffee. But I realized what it was, and this is just a recent realization. I met Dr. J a couple of weeks ago, and I was intimidated because most professional athletes are absolutely non-neurotic. If they have a bad game, they will not beat themselves up the way that I do after a performance.

That's interesting because when I was doing stand-up consistently, and had to be on the road three or four weeks in a row, I would never beat myself up after an event, because I remember Steve

Garvey saying, "You've got 162 games, so you can't ride an emotional roller coaster during a season." So I applied that to stand-up whenever I'd have a bad show. Recently I got up on stage and tried to do some old material and bombed. But I realized that I performed it poorly.

People don't understand that you can't do old material because it reflects something that you aren't anymore.

That's true, isn't it?

Yeah, you might as well be another comedian. If you can do your old material and make it work, you've got a bigger problem. That means you're stuck.

That's a good point.

It's a good thing to remember in a relationship, by the way.

How so?

You can't go, "Well, remember twenty years ago, we used to do this when we were happy?" You've got to be in the moment.

So you never really set out in life to be a comedian?

As I look back on it, it literally was a sublimated desire, but it makes complete sense that I ended up being a comedian because when I was ten, eleven, twelve, I was a funny little kid, and I was listening to comedy albums, and I knew comedians' routines when I was thirteen years old. So it makes complete sense. But I grew up in Tucson, Arizona, where there was no show business around, and I had no show business in my family, so I never thought, I'm going to be a comedian. But I used to watch every comedian on television that there was, and then I moved to L.A. to pursue a career. But I didn't have the courage to think of myself as a comedian and to go on stage. I don't have a performer's ego, I don't think. I think I'm more like a writer who is on his last legs.

Then what makes you want to go back to do it? Do you miss it?

I think I'm goal-oriented, which is opposite to the philosophy that I work at, which is just to work and have sort of no goals and no desires and let the rest take care of itself.

Zen.

Right. So I work really hard at that. But I have a desire to still do stand-up occasionally because I would like to do it right at some point.

You don't feel that you've done it right?

No, I think when I've done it right, I probably won't want to do it anymore. I don't know what it feels like to do it right, and if I'll ever have that feeling. I'm tortured, aren't I?

No, because I've wrestled with that too.

I feel I've seen you do it right. I want you to know that.

Jerry Seinfeld used to do three, four sets a night. Did you ever do that type of stuff?

No, I've never done anything three times a night.

Never?

No.

But I would think that you are driven in some respect because both of your TV shows are very individualistic and personal. There must be some drive that makes you put yourself through the grind, some drive for self-expression.

You're absolutely right. I am driven to fulfill some form of self-expression.

How did you decide to use Zen as a philosophy toward your performing?

Because I was so frightened on stage and so self-conscious, I thought, how does anyone become free? So I stumbled upon a book called *Zen and the Art of Archery,* and it talked about how Zen monks used archery as an exercise in self-awareness and enlightenment—the archers had to become goalless and not be thinking of the target. In the same way, I think that to be free in life, you can't constantly be thinking of the result.

There's also the thing of pulling your ego out.

Right, your ego can't be involved because it gets in the way of the process. So once I started to understand that your mind and ego get in the way of the process, I started to let go a little bit and became sort of more organic. Like a good piece of wheat bread.

That should be the title of your next special.

A Good Piece Of Wheat Bread?

A Good Piece Of Wheat Bread: The Organic Comedy of Garry Shandling.

That's a thought.

When we worked in San Diego, I noticed that your act changed some every night. Do you get bored doing the same material?

I get bored so quickly that I really don't like going on stage unless I have something new to try each time. Even if it's one joke.

Are you doing any stand-up now?

I went up on stage at The Comedy and Magic Club about three weeks ago for the first time in about six or eight months.

Were you rusty?

Yeah. I went up with a sheet of notes and just worked off of them.

How well-developed were the notes?

I'm a joke writer, so they're fairly well-constructed, but as I've gotten more experienced, I go up with a handful of concepts, and then I ad-lib on stage.

Were you nervous?

Yeah, but I cheat and go to a safe environment. I was at a club that I'm comfortable in, and it was kind of half out of town. I would be nervous getting up at, like, The Comedy Store where all the other comics were watching. That's like acting class. It's more frightening for me to do a scene in acting class with all the other actors watching than it is to actually do a scene in front of a camera because you can't fool the other actors.

I want to ask you about acceptance. Since you're accepted as a funny person by the public, does that help you develop your material, or does it hinder you by putting more pressure on you?

I think that acceptance is a springboard to go deeper, because once the audience accepts that you're funny, you no longer have to prove that. You're now freer to explore.

SINBAD

"If I Ain't Quick Enough To Make People Laugh Without Cursing . . . "

Sinbad is that rare comedian who doesn't have to prepare before he goes on stage. He has complete trust in his comedic instincts. He just trusts himself to be funny when the time comes—and he is. He's also a man who has a tremendous amount of energy and drive. Years ago, Sinbad opened for me at a college in Delaware. After the show, we talked till four in the morning, and I could tell even then that, with his drive, sense of humor, and personality, it was going to take a lot to hold him back from success. I had the extremely good-natured and effervescent Sinbad speak to my class because I wanted them to hear from a successful comedian who is the exception to the rule of extensively preparing the material, and how he goes about not preparing, so to speak. This question-and-answer session was conducted at my class in the summer of 1992.

SINBAD

You're not really a material-oriented comedian, are you?

No. I really should sit down and write more, but I've been lucky because it just comes to me.

How so?

I see my jokes. I'm about to go on stage, and say I'm going to talk about swimming and that's all I have. And I just see myself swimming and I see other people I've known swimming, and when I get on stage, it just happens.

So you just kind of get into your imagination?

Absolutely. I just go off on it.

You say you just go off with the subject matter, but have you thought this through at one time, and then said, "I'll use that?"

No, it just comes out of me. Luckily, I have a memory. I can remember back when I was three or four years old. I remember my first swimming lesson. And I remember it in detail. All you do in comedy is take real life and split it enough so that it'll go up. Make it something that you really didn't do, but you could have.

So you don't write at all?

I'll write and then I'll lose my notes. No, really, I'll find something I really like, put it down on a napkin or piece of paper, and put it in my pocket. Then right before I go on stage, I might look at it. But if something else occurs to me, I'll go with that. Like I was moving into a new house, and watching my father help me move was tripping me out. I said, That's my next bit, my father moving. And I didn't have to write it, because he did it. So I write down "my father moving." And not the joke.

Can you tell the same story twice?

It changes all the time. You add to it, and it moves, and it should. Because you have a new audience every night, you can become very lazy as a comic. That's why we have to push ourselves to create new material.

Say you're working on the road and one night you come up with a very good routine that really works all the way through. How much of it will you use the next night without changing it?

I would use it the next night, and then something would grow on it. Because the game I play with myself is, make it grow. Nobody else in the room has to know this. My game is to keep the waitresses looking and listening to me every night—because the waitresses that work at comedy clubs are your judge of comedy. My goal is, if you saw me twice, you got something different the next time.

When do you set something that gets a strong reaction so that it becomes a strong part of your repertoire?

If it's strong and I like it, I just keep doing it.

And how much will it change?

I don't know exactly, but it will change until the day I don't do it anymore.

Do you ever have any reluctance at letting a good bit go?

You can't be scared to get rid of stuff, and you can't limit yourself. I've seen comics say that they can't think of anything to talk about, and I say, "Just walk outside and look." I used to go to emergency rooms and bus stops. Man, the craziest people in the world ride the bus, and I'd just watch them. I would ride the busses. That why I think a comic's worst enemy is success. Because now the limo picks you up, now you stay out in a gated community, and you tell people, "Get that for me, go pick that up." And now you've become your own worst enemy. That's why you see comics explode when they become successful. Comics were made to be gypsies. We weren't made to be contained. We're not supposed to be able to come to a board meeting.

So you think we're all rebellious in nature?

Yeah. We're not supposed to be the guy that they go, "He's so nice, he just does what you tell him." We're supposed to be the one where they go, "We had the camera on him, but he might not go the way you think he's going."

Since you've always had such a freewheeling approach, did you bomb much when you started?

No, man, to be honest, I never bombed on stage. One night a crowd booed me, because they wanted to see the SOS Band, and the SOS Band didn't show up. Fifteen thousand people out there waiting, and I told the emcee, "Don't tell them that the SOS Band is not here." The minute he walks out there, it's, "Ladies and gentlemen, we regret to say the SOS Band is not here."

Did you open for a lot of musical acts in the early stages of your career?

Oh yeah. We used to get those gigs for $50. When a black concert would come to town, they would come to the comedy club. "Somebody's got to open for Smokey Robinson. You got any black comics?" Me, me, me. That's how I got started. And then when I got to the concert, they had the lowest guy on the totem pole in charge of me. And I had my little clothes in a bag, and found out there was no dressing room. So I'd find myself a corner and change. And what happened is that I felt so bad, I went on stage, and said, Man, they don't know it, but I'm somebody. Boom. And I killed.

Did you have anything prepared?

I told the audience that I read the newspapers, so what do you want me to talk about? And I'll never forget that first night: Somebody wanted me to talk about ballet, and luckily I had just gone to a ballet the day before. And the reason the woman asked me to talk about it is because she saw me sitting at the ballet eating this candy that I had snuck in. So I did this whole ballet scene.

Have you ever been nervous on stage?

My most nervous moment was when I had to do a gig at an old-folks' show. And there was a man who sat in the audience the whole time and just looked at me. And his wife was laughing, and he was looking at me. I said, "Man, what are you, deaf?" She said, "Yes, he is." Well, the audience just gasped. And I said, "He's lucky, because he doesn't have to hear you nagging." And she said it to him, and he cracked up. And it saved me.

Did you become a comedian because people were always telling you that you were funny?

No, people used to call me stupid. Like in college when I'd make 'em laugh, they'd say, "Hey man, you stupid." So I said, "Yeah, I think I'll be a comic because I'm stupid."

Was going to college a help or hindrance to your development as a comedian?

Definitely a help for me because you need college and all those other experiences in life to make you funny. I think when people start out as comics at thirteen, sixteen, seventeen years old, they miss a lot of life. Because I think you have to live to be funny. You have to have had a regular job. You have to have been fired from jobs. You have to have had a landlord come get your money from you, to have been kicked out of places. It's strange but to be a comic you need a lot of negativity. You don't see many rich kids become great comedians. Normally, people who haven't had the car, the women, who weren't very popular become comics.

Your act is one of the cleanest around. Have you ever used profanity in a show?

The first time I did a show—I guess this goes back to the question of whether I've bombed—after I got out of the military was in Illinois. I was on stage trying to find myself, just talking. And all these guys had just been on cussing ahead of me. So I'm on stage, it wasn't working, and I cussed a couple of times. They laughed at the curse words, and I walked out of the place and thought, If I ain't quick enough to make people laugh without cursing, I quit. See, cursing by itself is not bad; it's when you ain't got nothing to say. So you stop. Look at Richard Pryor. Let's look at the man who we wish we all could be like. Richard was a genius. It wasn't cursing that made him famous. People forgot when he was clean. He was a clean comic and walked off the stage in Vegas back to the chitlin circuit. He believed in himself so much that he gave up success and had to start all over again. So when these young kids talk about Richard, I say, "We need to read about Richard."

GEORGE WALLACE

"They're Buying Me"

George Wallace is both literally and figuratively one of the larger-than-life comedians. He just takes over a stage and, with his infectious personality and smile, he commandeers the audience to go along on his comedic trip. A confessed comedy workaholic, George is always in perpetual motion and rarely at home. But wherever he is, he's not far from a stage—four days away from a stage is about as long as he can take. One of his most interesting revelations is that, even though Spain is one of George's favorite places to vacation, even when traveling halfway across the world, he'll only go for four days. Then it's back to America and the comedy stage. This interview with the jovial and peripatetic Mr. Wallace was conducted at The Buzz Café on Sunset Boulevard in July 1996.

GEORGE WALLACE

George, how long have you been doing stand-up comedy?

Twenty years this month: 1976. I went to The Comic Strip in New York City and Catch a Rising Star.

What were you doing before you tried stand-up? Someone told me you were in advertising—

Yeah, vice president of the world's largest outdoor advertising agency in New York City. All of the spectacle at Times Square, the billboards, 5000 busses in New York City—the ten top markets in America: Boston, Detroit, Philadelphia, Los Angeles, San Francisco. I was vice president of that market. And I loved it. I made a lot of money. The reason I went into advertising before show business was because when I'd see comics on television, they'd talk about how when they first started, they didn't know where their next meal was coming from, so I decided that I didn't want any part of that. I wanted to make a lot of money to get a financial cushion.

So you did not want to do the suffering-artist route?

No sir.

But you knew even then that you wanted to go into show business?

Yes sir. I've joked that I wanted to be a comedian before I was born because I didn't come out of my mother's womb until the doctor said, "Five minutes, Mr. Wallace."

When were you first aware of that desire?

Ever since I was six years old and saw Red Skelton on TV.

Really? Red Skelton was your first influence?

Red Skelton is the reason I'm in the business. Playing all the characters that he did. Then about seventh grade through the twelfth grade, I'd sneak in the room and listen to my parents' albums by Redd Foxx, Pigmeat Markham, and Moms Mabley. That's when I really solidified the fact that I wanted to be a comedian, because I took their jokes to school the next day and became not the class clown, but certainly the class comedian.

Did your teachers ever suggest that you should become a comedian?

No, I come from a little school in Atlanta, Georgia, called Linwood Park High School. Nobody knew anything about show business. So that was the furthest thing from our minds on career day. We had the Wonder Bread man, the Charles potato-chip man, and the milk man come do our school. We didn't have any stockbrokers or anybody like that. But we were talking about careers.

Did going to college help you as a comedian or not?

Yes, for different reasons. In school I was a dorm counselor, and you learn a lot just by basically learning to live with people from all over the world. Because that's all I do now—interact with people. And that's what I was doing in college. And I never would have learned that, because I come from a little black community in Atlanta.

What college did you go to?

University of Akron in Akron, Ohio. Twenty thousand students and not even one percent black at that time. But I grew up never knowing too much about race stuff, so whatever I wanted to do, I fit in.

You were just kind of able to fit in—

Yeah, I became a part of it. Like you were supposed to be a dorm counselor after three years of college, but I was one after one quarter.

Which leads me to a question regarding your career. For years you opened for Tom Jones, and I always found it interesting that you were a black comedian opening up for a white superstar, and a white audience. That's pretty rare in the business, isn't it?

It is very rare. It's interesting that you brought that up because I just like people so much that I don't even know what I'm doing. But it is different. I was able to open for this man for five years and be accepted by his audience. Which is ninety-nine and a half percent white. And I never thought about being black or anything like that.

Never thought about it?

No, but I never thought about that when I was doing advertising in New York City, a little black person walking into some guy's office and asking him for $100,000 for an advertising program. Then one day it hit me, say, like I bet one of those guys is going like, "Look at this little nigger coming in here to ask me for $100,000. He must be crazy." Then on the other side, I'm thinking, like, "I'm going to work with this guy, so it all evens out either way."

Even though you came from a black community in Georgia, you were raised in a color-blind way?

Yeah, I was raised in a color-blind way.

Even though you were in the South?

Yeah, but my parents are white, let's get that straight. [Laughter] No, I was brought up color-blind. My parents were okay. My dad had a second-grade education. And I think my mom stayed in school a week longer than he did. But they made out. My dad was the man of the neighborhood.

Did you interact much with whites in Georgia when you were growing up?

Only the people I worked with. I was the first black to operate the cash register in my neighborhood and stuff like that. So I never had a problem with people. And I still don't. That's my job.

I can't think of another black comedian who has opened for a popular white act.

Yeah, I did a lot of people. I opened for Helen Reddy, Paul Anka, hell, I opened up for The Beach Boys.

How did you end up opening for those people? Did you have to go after those gigs?

I had an agent, and I just think the word got around that this kid is clean, he's a pleasant surprise, and he's black. They would always say, "And he's black. But he can do it."

Has race played any part in the development or non-development of your career in your mind?

I think it's stopped me from getting in some doors, but I think it's helped me get in some doors. It always plays a part, but I don't dwell on that because I feel it balances out.

Did your background in marketing help you build your career?

I think it does. That's what I do now when I'm in different cities. I take advantage of radio and television. I'm up at six in the morning doing the early-morning radio and television. At noon I do the mid-day news. People see me on stage for an hour, but they don't know I flew all night to get there and went right from the airport to a radio station.

Do you thrive on that type of pace or does it tire you out?

It's really good to me. I need to occupy my time doing something.

Over the years you played in a lot of different-sized venues. How did you learn to adapt to them?

That's one reason that I was never in a hurry to become a successful comedian overnight, because I wanted to learn how to become a comedian. My first show was with Natalie Cole with 17,000 people outside, outdoors. I've worked in the round, in theaters, dinner theaters, proscenium-arch theaters. So now, it's no problem. George Wallace can work in any venue: 300 people, 30,000, I know how to do it.

You seem to strike me generally as someone who doesn't have stage fright. Did you feel at home on stage from the very first?

I think I always felt at home just making people happy. Even during college days I always like being in the leader position.

So there's no angst associated with performing for you?

No, that's my most comfortable moment. It's my sex and drugs. I get off on stage. Like a lot of entertainers run around trying to get a piece of ass, but my ass is on stage. I really love what I do.

Well, if that's the way you feel, how were you able to defer starting your comedy career for so long?

I wanted to make some money first, but I made sure that I did get to New York, which was the most important thing for a comedian to do. And it still is important for a comedian to start in New York.

Why more so than Los Angeles?

The competitiveness. Everything is competitive in New York City, and the work ethic is different. Everybody's going out every night. Here they're trying to do one show a week. We were trying to do four shows a night. That's why all the best comedians still come from the East Coast. When they come here, they're used to doing four sets a night. You have a guy in New York and the joker ain't funny, but three weeks from now he'll know what he did wrong, and he'll sharpen it up some way.

Are you a disciplined writer?

No, I'm not. That's my answer, but that may not be my friends' answer, because they'll tell you that I'm writing shit down every day. Every five minutes. You say something, and I'm writing it down. So I'm not a disciplined writer whereas I sit down and write out bits, but I am a disciplined writer where I note my observations. I've got little pieces of paper all over the house. I've got drawers, boxes, all kinds of stuff with just little napkins and matchbook covers.

Do you throw any of it out?

Only after I document it.

When you say document it, what do you mean?

Put it on your legal pad. You know, I'm known for a legal pad, too. I walk up on stage with a legal pad, when I'm doing new jokes. I transfer it from the napkin to the legal pad, and then I walk on stage and say that I've got some new jokes, might be funny, might not, but I don't give a shit, I'm going to try them out either way.

Do you feel that admission brings the audience along with you?

They're feeling like, the guy's being honest. I'll do a joke and it works real good. I'll write that down: "Worked real good." They like it. Do another joke that misses. "Needs work." The audience loves that. I'll do another joke that I think is funny that the audience didn't think was funny, and I'll write "audience sucks." They love that.

You're doing this while you're on stage?

This is while I'm on stage, yeah.

And that kind of brings them into the act, and helps you save any joke that doesn't work at the same time?

It doesn't matter. They're getting off—saying, We'll help with the joke. Or they just feel comfortable with me being honest about, Did the joke work, does it need work?

Will you do this in a concert or just at The Improv?

People want this done everywhere, but I only do it at my workout places. But Arsenio insisted that I do that one night on his TV show. And Jay Leno wants me to do it, too. So one night, I'm going to walk out there with the yellow pad.

Why do they want you to do it?

It's just funny to see someone out there being honest, doing a joke that bombs, and then you still get a laugh. Like I say, once again, that goes right back to my personality that I'm conveying.

Let's talk about your working methods. What's your way of developing material?

My way of developing material is really to just see something and say it. It's basically my personality. When I walk on stage, it's basically me you're buying. You're not buying any particular joke, or anything like that. You're buying George Wallace. My point of view is that I'm relaying a message that you would like to extend yourself.

Do you feel a strong need to say the things that you observe?

Yeah, and it doesn't matter what it is. I'm usually pretty right on the money with what people are thinking. Like I talk about foreign aid today. You know, I don't like foreign aid. I do like it, but in the back of my head, I'm thinking, We give every Tom, Dick, and Harry money, and we can't even take care of Washington, D.C. And I'll give an opinion like that. And then I'll go on to foreign countries like Bosnia Herznia—as a matter of fact, if we can't pronounce your name, you ain't getting shit.

So coming from your own belief on an issue, you find out if people agree with your thinking?

Yeah. I am so basic that people stop and think, Yeah, that does make sense. It's like when people say to me, "He's just as nice as he wants to be." I'll think, What the hell does that mean? What if I come over there and slap the shit out of you? People say, "What you do that for?" I'll say, "Well, that's just as nice as I want to be today." I'm always looking at the absurd, and I listen to everything. I'll take any point that anybody says and just twist it around.

So your antenna is always out?

That's how I work.

Were you always like this or is this something you developed?

It's something I developed in the last twenty years. Because that's my job. Let's make that clear. My job is to have the antennas out. I've been on *The Tonight Show* for twenty years, but you can't continue to do *The Tonight Show* for twenty years and not have the antennas out because you got to keep them with new stuff. That's the difference in the comedians who do a lot of TV and those who don't—new jokes.

Is it easier to do *The Tonight Show* with Jay than it was with Johnny Carson?

Are you kidding? I only did *The Tonight Show* with Johnny one time. I don't think he liked me. Jay is just real easy to do the show with. They don't even check my material anymore, they just ask me what I'm gonna do. The problem with me is that I don't know what I'm gonna do till I get there, and then when I tell them what I wanna do, I won't do it. But it works anyway. That's the magic of the show.

What's the key to doing well on *The Tonight Show*?

It's very important to watch and listen to everything that's happening when you're on the show. That's your opening. The last time I did the show I was the number two guest, and there were a lot of superstars on the show doing cameo appearances. The audience stood up for each of them, so when I walked out, I said "You stood up for everyone else, stand up for me too." So the next clubs I did, when I walked out on stage, I got standing ovations. I still don't realize the power of television. I don't know why people are looking at me sometimes and saying hi. I forget that I'm on television. And a black man is more visible on TV than a white man. I can get away with doing *The Tonight Show* twice a year. People are always saying, "I saw you on television last week." Because I make such a strong statement.

Are you totally comfortable on television?

Very much so. And the more I do it, the more comfortable I get.

Any difference in the way you feel doing panel or stand-up?

You have to be better doing panel than stand-up because that's your personal moment. You're delivering jokes in a different manner. I don't have to do panel nowadays because people know George Wallace as a stand-up, but it is very important that comedians continue to do stand-up. You can't think that just because you have a TV show that you should just do panel. People will forget what you do and you won't be able to sell tickets to your live appearances. They'll see your name on the marquee and say, "He's on television, but what does he do?" That's why Jerry Seinfeld still stands up. He lets people know that that's what he does—he does stand-up. As big as Cosby and Carlin are, they still walk out there and do stand-up.

Will you do *The Tonight Show* on short notice?

Don't ever let them call you to do the show tomorrow unless you're really prepared, because you must make sure that you score big. Even as good as I think I am, if I'm not really prepared and I go over there and don't do as well as I did the last time, they'll forget that they just called you yesterday. They'll just remember that you didn't do as well as before. Every shot is like the Super Bowl.

Would you say your personality dominates your material?

Without a doubt. Some of these new guys, anybody can do their jokes. There's the new black one, and there's the new white one, and it doesn't matter. The new black ones, all they can talk about is fucking, and the new white ones are doing their generic how-come-you-never whatever. But I'm trying to get better. I have my tricks, but I'm still learning.

What are you still learning?

Like in Birmingham last week, I went slower than I normally do, and the people were still laughing. And I realized that going that slow I was able to do half the jokes I normally do. That showed me that there's always a reason to change and do it differently. I'm still learning how to deal with different audiences. Today I'm working for ninety percent white audiences, tomorrow ninety percent black. The next day mixed.

How do you make that adjustment in your material or act?

I can do the same show, just deliver it differently. I can do that in different ways, even if I were to go South.

Tell me about that a little bit.

For instance, if I go down South, the dialect is a little different, and I can talk about more Southern things and present it in a Southern way. As opposed to if I were to go onstage in New York, then I'd come across a little differently.

So you actually make regional shifts in your delivery?

Very much so. And a big regional shift in Las Vegas.

Why is that?

Because it's perhaps the toughest audience in America.

Because they're not concentrating?

Yeah, and they're not regional. If you go to Atlantic City, you got the eastern corridor, you go down South, you got Southern comedy, but when you go to Las Vegas, people are from everywhere. I've been on stage in Vegas with 400 people in the room not even laughing.

When was that?

That was with Tom Jones at Caesar's Palace, but I'm so comfortable with working on that stage that I just stopped the show. And I found out I had 400 Japanese. But at least I found out what was going on. Then I acknowledged them. And then one night we had some people from India. And I said, "Where you from, New Delhi?" Then I did some simple thing like, They just opened up a new deli around the corner. If you acknowledge them, it makes your show better, and they can start laughing.

Can you break down for me some of the things that you've learned in twenty years of doing stand-up?

Seventeen years ago right here at The Comedy Store we used to practice heckling each other so that we could practice our responses. I learned how to start, how to wrap up.

What's your rule on how to start?

First thing you'd better do is sell yourself. Put your personality out first, ask the audience how they're doing. 'Cause there's no reason for you to buy Coke over Pepsi; you've gotta like the salesperson who's selling it.

Give me your rule on wrapping up your show.

You better be doing your best stuff at that time, 'cause there's a reason to close. The best compliment you can get when you come off stage is for people to say, "I enjoyed that." Even if they say, "You started off a little slow, but you came on at the end and kicked some ass." You don't want them to say that you started off good, but at the end you kind of petered out.

If your show changes each night, and you want to end strong each night, do you have four or five different chunks of strong closing material?

Yes I do. I can close anywhere down the line.

So you're very comfortable in all situations on stage?

If it's difficult, then I want to try it. Many times I'll come up on stage at The Improv, Comedy Store, or Laff Factory, and comics'll say that the audience sucks, and I'll tell the audience, "Well, all the other comedians say y'all suck, and it's a shitty audience, so I've got some shitty jokes here and since you're a shitty audience, this should work out pretty good." So, all of a sudden, now, they're loosened up.

Is this fearlessness in your approach to stand-up just a part of your nature?

Yeah, it came from my dad.

A strong self-esteem?

Yeah.

So did you ever bomb when you started?

I bombed one time so bad at the Neverly Hotel, an all-Jewish resort. I was just starting, and I was doing borrowed jokes, and whatever joke I did they had already heard it. I was just not ready. I had been on stage for forty-five minutes, and I don't think I got half a laugh. But I did stay up there. I bombed so bad that when I was driving back, I wanted to drive off the bridge. I mean, it hurt so bad, but what I learned from that is that if I bomb again, it will never be as bad as that night. And that's why you learn something every time you go on stage. And I went back to the Neverly two years later, and this white lady with gray hair comes up to me and says, "I remember the first time you came, you got no laughs, but now you're much better."

Did that bombing experience make you think about quitting at that time?

No, the best thing for a comedian to do is to get on stage as soon as possible, and that's what can happen in New York City. You can bomb, but you can be on stage the next night, three or four times.

Were you back on stage the next night?

The very next night.

Was your confidence shaken?

It's amazing what happens when you get on stage: All of a sudden you're back on stage, and it doesn't matter. It's completely new. It's like you can be sick, but when you go on stage and get the mike in your hand, everything leaves. There's a shot of adrenaline and you just go at it.

Adrenaline. Maybe that's what it is.

That's what it is. Especially when it's your drug.

Would you write bad checks to perform? Would you sell a TV to get on stage?

That's a crazy question, but I'd do anything to get on stage. Right now, they're giving me lots of money to work, but the fact of the matter is that I would do it for free. I would do it for free. No doubt about it.

Let's talk a little about *Def Comedy Jam*. Are you going to host that?

Yeah, I'm going to do that because I think it's time. Nobody's done it like that before. It's been basically a blue show.

Have you been approached to do that show before?

Not to do it, but to host it. I've never been their cup of tea as far as that mode of comedy.

Do you have any profanity in your act?

Nothing but a little "shit" here and "damn" there. But I'm going to do it my way, just so the other black comics know that there is another way.

Do you feel that the idea that you can be clever and funny without being gratuitously vulgar has been lost in black comedians?

What happened was that Richard Pryor did it better than anybody else. And then Eddie Murphy came along, and went a little over Richard's way. And then the younger people topped Eddie and didn't listen to Richard. Richard was blue, but Richard always had some kind of insight.

Now you've got some good young black comedians out there too. But what has happened is that the young ones think, "I've gotta get to television," and the only way to get to television really quick for a black comedian is *Def Comedy Jam*. Where you and I were looking at *The Tonight Show*, they're looking at *Def Comedy Jam*. But I think that's going to change in the next few years because even the African-American community is saying, "I've heard enough obscenity."

Tell me about the time you were at a club in New York and you did a set on a *Def Comedy Jam* night, and the reaction of the young black comics who saw your set.

I was at Caroline's in New York and I wanted to try out some material for a *Letterman* spot, and they went berserk enjoying it. They wanted to know how I could be that funny in a clean way.

How did you answer them?

By being George Wallace, and finding out who you are as a comedian. And that takes between seven and eleven years.

How do you follow a series of comedians doing a lot of profanity and sexually oriented material with your style of comedy?

Enough people know me, and I know that I'm sharp enough after twenty years to know that now it's my show and my stage no matter what happened before me. It might take me three minutes, but I'll change the mood of the room.

So your first step is to change the mood of the room?

Yeah, because you have to get everything off that stage that came before you.

How do you do that?

I'll talk to the audience a little. Ask them how they're doing. I might be going a little slow, but I'm changing the mood. Another one of my tricks is to compliment the comedian before me, especially if he killed.

So you actually come in at an energy a little less than normal, and then bring it up?

Right. Because no matter what you do, it's probably gonna be your last ten minutes that's going to leave the strongest impression.

So how you close the show is the most important thing?

Right, how you close the show.

Then how do you work the order of your routine? Does it change every night?

Every night my show is different, and I don't throw away anything, so there's a possibility you could hear a joke tonight that I did twenty years ago. That's why my audience keeps coming back, because I change the act quite a bit.

Do you ever get tired of doing a joke?

Sometimes I don't get tired of it, but I think that the audience might've heard it already.

Do you have a lot of repeat customers at your shows?

Always. Every city I go to, people come up and tell me, "We've been here every time you come here, and you always have a different show."

Do you every worry about repeating your jokes for people who have heard them already?

I know I'm always doing so much new material that the chances are slim.

How long a show are you doing these days?

An hour to an hour and fifteen minutes.

No matter what venue?

In clubs, I go to an hour and twenty. But really I have no business being on longer than fifty minutes. Fifty minutes to an hour, I don't care how funny you are, it's time to go.

Do you have a pre-show ritual?

I write down what I'm going to do every night on my pad, because I know my act, but I really don't, because I'm trying to throw in new jokes each night. So I have to remind myself that this joke or that joke has to go in there.

Do you tape your shows every night?

I taped last week, but I haven't listened to it.

So you've never been big on taping your show?

I started out taping, but I lost so many tape recorders I couldn't afford it.

Is it possible for anyone to become a comedian?

That's a good question. I think it is for anyone who wants to become one, but it's one of the toughest jobs in the world because there's more bullshit in show business than anywhere else. But you gotta want to do it, and if you're determined to do something, then nothing can stop you.

JONATHAN WINTERS
"My Comedy Is With Me Constantly"

The words "improvisational comedy genius" and Jonathan Winters have long been synonymous to both the comedy aficionado and the casual observer of comedians. Recently awarded the prestigious Mark Twain Award for humor by the Kennedy Center for the Performing Arts, Jonathan Winters is the epitome of the improvisational stand-up—without a doubt the most difficult and daring form of stand-up (proven by the fact that, with the exception of Robin Williams, virtually no other contemporary comedian attempts it with any regularity).

I first met Jonathan Winters in November of 1988. I had been signed to perform on a Showtime special entitled *Jonathan Winters and Friends*. I was glad that I had been in the business for sixteen year before I met Jonathan because it enabled me to meet him with feelings of great respect but not awe. This allowed me to make a more objective assessment of his great talents when I watched him work. I had been a big fan of his style of humor since I was a kid, but like most viewers, I just took in the totality of his humor without really understanding how he did it, yet instinctively knowing that I couldn't do it.

Since Jonathan had been relatively inactive for a number of years, there had not been many opportunities to watch him in top form, because that is also part and parcel of improvisation—there is a hit-and-miss quality even among the greatest practitioners. But during the taping of this particular Showtime special, Jonathan was on his game. And Jonathan Winters with his game together is really a sight to behold. Just like in athletics, the more weapons you have, the better you can compensate when one aspect of your game isn't there. Well, Jonathan has infinite comedic resources. He has eyes that can go from sad to impish in an instant. When his lines aren't necessarily funny, his faces, voices, sound effects, or body movements will step up to keep you laughing. He's able to synthesize the elements of speed and space, so that even though he's moving fast, there's a bit of space or pause, which gives him a thoughtful quality as well. While Robin Williams is more frenetic and one-line-oriented, Jonathan is slower and more character-oriented in his improvisations. He creates three-dimensional people (like Maude Frickert) who seem to take on lives of their own, and the dialogue that he gives them has a subtlety and depth that's both exquisite and daunting.

Watching Jonathan that night, I couldn't help but wonder, "How could anyone this hip come out of Dayton, Ohio?" Having formed a friendship with Jonathan, and had my answering machine be the recipient of his long, zany messages, it was with this question in mind that I interviewed him at his home in 1990.

JONATHAN WINTERS

When people talk about improvisation, your name is always the first one mentioned.

Well it should be. [Laughs] It's the only time my ego comes out. Not that I invented it, but I was in the race, so to speak. I feel that when the gun went off, I at least got a good start on the rest of the dudes.

I first became aware of you in about 1960 when you had a show on CBS in which you would take an item and improvise a routine around it for the last seven minutes of the show. You were the first comedian that I had ever seen do that. Had there been one previous to you who influenced you?

Interestingly enough, two of the strongest guys who influenced me were not performers but writers. One was O. Henry, and the other was James Thurber. I grew up in Ohio, and James Thurber grew up in Ohio. We were a couple of Buckeyes. I have all of James Thurber's books. His characters were very Midwestern, but when he painted these characters in his books, they really came to life. I think regardless of one's background or race, you could identify with the grandfather and the grandmother or the kids, and O. Henry and Thurber gave great twists to the ends of their stories.

Could you predict the endings?

No, and that's what I wanted to do with my comedy. I've always believed this: You gotta take more chances. You gotta be a gambler in your material. You're gonna get your hands spanked every now and then, but you're also gonna get some, "Hey, I loved what the guy said. I wonder if he said that off the top of his head."

You must have been influenced by radio then.

Oh yeah. I loved radio because of the imagination.

Is the video age stripping us of our imagination rather than enhancing it?

Although I grew up with radio, a great chunk of my life obviously has been television, and I think in many cases we've done a terrible injustice to a lot of people. I know that a lot of people in our country can't read and write, but to talk to people who can read and write today is frightening. I think our libraries for the most part are at Vons and Safeway in the wire brackets near the check-out counter. *The Star, People* magazine and the *National Enquirer* are the literature of today.

How do you view the risk of offending people with your comedy?

I've always tried—and it's been a thing with me 'cause I know how I'd feel—to never out and out offend people.

But in gambling with your material, that's always a risk, isn't it?

It's always a risk, but it comes down to the individual comedian's sensitivity to people. For example, the older I get, the more I understand why a black guy might feel the way he does about my portraying a black character. If I do a football guy, he can rightfully say, "Some of us aren't into football, some of us are artists, some of us are scientists, some of us are jet flyers." What was told to me was, "If you are to do me, then give me some dignity, give me some strength, man. Don't put me with that broom." That's improvisation.

When you do a show like *The Tonight Show*, do you speak to anyone from the staff before the show?

I give them a list of questions to ask me. For example, I'll tell them to ask me about living on a farm, and then I'll improvise a response.

Say you're improvising and it's not going well. Does the lack of laughter start to inhibit your creative mechanisms?

I think it's like a fighter—a smart fighter . . . which I'm not. If a fighter is going a few rounds with a fighter whose style is awkward for him, if he's smart he's got to change his style. For me it's a strange thing.

Can you change your style?

Uh-uh. I'm locked in. I'm gonna have to go with it, I've got no place to go, and I gotta pick up that check best I can, even if the guy says, "Here, take this, I'll never hire you again."

Given your penchant for improvisation, when it comes to film work and staying with what is written, is that difficult for you?

I'd say in ninety-eight percent of the film work I adhered to the script. If you get carried away and start to wander in your dialogue, the people who get uptight are the other actors. Very few people can improvise; they're locked into the script. So I have to stay with the script.

Are you a quick study of the lines?

No. I really have to work hard. It doesn't come to me. There are no tricks. I can't work with a tape recorder as most actors do. In my prayers I've always said, "Oh God, please make me a quick study." Jackie Gleason and Mickey Rooney are guys who could look through twenty-five pages for few moments and then say, "Okay, let's go out and shoot it." But those are the only ones I've seen who can do that.

Which do you prefer: live performing or film work?

There's nothing like a live performance. However, if you were to ask me if I'd rather be on a stage in Atlantic City or Vegas or if I'd rather be in a good movie with a good script, good director, and good people, I'd have to say I'd rather be in that movie. A good movie will be seen all over the world. Plus, I've always been a movie buff.

Do you still get nervous before a live performance?

Yeah, I get nervous. Not to the extent where I'm looking for a bucket to throw up in, but realize that I'm going out there on raw power and I'm trying to get my thoughts together. The toughest time for me is the first couple of minutes. I've known Bill Cosby for a long time, and I asked him if he got nervous before a performance. He said, "I don't sweat it. What's to get nervous about?"

Are you as active a performer as you'd like?

Pretty much as I'd like. I would like to be doing some more pictures, but I realize that I'm not a kid anymore. I'm sixty-four years of age, and there's only a small number of parts that I'm gonna be offered—usually fifty-five to sixty-five—and that's okay. I'm doing pretty much what I want to do. I'm writing and I paint.

How would you characterize the different self-expression needs that the writing, painting, and comedy meet for you?

My comedy is with me constantly. My comedy is number one, painting number two, and the writing is third. It's tough for me to discipline myself to write, and I just paint when I feel like it.

Whereas with my comedy, I've found that even when I'm not making a cent, I might go into a restaurant and pull this out [Winters pulls a police badge out of his back pocket], show it to a stranger, and say, "You're the man we're looking for, please come along with me."

Why do you carry a police badge?

Because I use it. My difficulty, Franklyn, is I forget that not everybody has a sense of humor and that not everyone is tuned into my little world. I like to have what I think of as innocent fun and play with the people around me on a daily basis wherever I am. And I get corrected, and that's okay because it's all part of improvisation, of taking a chance. Now the thing I love about painting is that I'm in charge.

And you don't feel that with the comedy?

No, 'cause somebody's always gonna correct you. Someone's gonna tell you that you've only got so many minutes. Same thing with the movies. When I've got the canvas and the palette I can go to work and paint what I want. It may not sell or it may sell. It doesn't make any difference. Same thing with my writing. When I wrote my book, I just thought, Wouldn't it be something if I just got it published, wouldn't it be great to get a cover on that son of a gun. It became a bestseller.

I heard that Gorbachev read it as part of perestroika.

Perestroika? That's funny place over there. A friend of mine visited that place, perestroika. You know what it is? It's like our Magic Mountain. It's about one hundred ten miles north of Moscow. The most popular ride is the giant shoe.

How do you feel about the fact that, for the most part, comedians are considered jesters?

I think that's good. I think it's healthy, as long as you don't get carried away. I try to be informative. It's fascinating to me to throw in some history with some out-and-out farce.

It seems like the sixties were a period when cerebral point-of-view comedy started its appearance with Lenny Bruce, Mort Sahl, Bob Newhart, etcetera. Did you go watch these people?

Sure. Because we were all basically fighting for the same thing. To be different, say something a little offbeat. Lenny certainly did. Shelly Berman was very active then. Dick Gregory was coming along at that time.

Who was the funniest to you at that time?

Lenny was awfully funny. He was just starting the four-letter-word stuff. He thought funny.

How long was a typical engagement in the late fifties and early sixties?

About seven days, two shows a night.

Did that get repetitious?

It all depends on the audience, who you're working for. If they treat you right, and the people out front treat you right, you look forward to coming to work.

How many minutes were you doing when you headlined a place like the Hungry I in San Francisco?

About forty-five.

Were those totally improvised shows at that time?

When I was drinking, I had moments of improvisation, but I was very locked into certain bits. I wouldn't take any chances. Soon as

I got sober, I got freer. Giving up the sauce put me in charge. Then I could think again for the first time.

Did your family travel with you when you were actively on the road?

Now and then. My wife would come with me to Tahoe, which I played in the summer. They'd give me a house, so my wife would invite her mother down, and I'd have the kids and they'd be jumping in the lake. Meanwhile, I'd be sitting in my room thinking about what I was gonna do that night.

Did you find it hard to relax on the days that you had a show?

Yeah, 'cause the whole seven days that I'd be in that place I couldn't enjoy myself. There's no relaxing for me. It's all work. I gotta think, I gotta be sharp. From time to time people have asked me, "Why did you quit clubs?" It was kinda simple for me. It took a long time for it to sink in, but when it did it became simple: A performer gets up for the first show, then you get up for the second show, and then it's over. I can't speak for those people who are taking drugs, or smoking something, or taking sauce, 'cause I can't take that 'cause of mental problems that I've had, but for me it became a question of, How do you get back down? I thought for a time I couldn't get back down. I couldn't get to sleep until about five a.m.

What was the last straw?

I think that basically all along I just wanted to be home. I had my kids to raise. I saw my boy letter in sports, and my girl do her little funny dances in school, and I'm glad I did. If you don't want to have kids, that's fine, but I wanted children, and I think that if you're gonna have kids, the least you can do is be there.

Do you still watch comedy and comedians?

Oh yeah. When a guy is funny, he's funny. As trite or corny as it might sound, outside of sex, to me the greatest high is laughing.

You sit back there and the guy just takes you through a scene, and, man, if you're into his way of thinking, into his mind, and he's painted a picture that you can identify with, you're on a trip with him. A lot of the effect is created by the picture that you can create.

One last question: Other than you, how many hip people were there in Dayton, Ohio?

Twenty-seven .

Part III

SEARCHING FOR TALENT

All comedians arrive by trial and error.
—Groucho Marx

BUDD FRIEDMAN
(Club Owner, The Improv)

Gerson "Budd" Friedman is the owner of the world-famous Improv in Los Angeles and has been on hand at the birth of many of America's greatest stand-up comedians. Budd first owned The Improv in New York, but lost it to his first wife in a divorce settlement. He then came to Los Angeles, took over the site of the old Ash Grove club on Melrose Boulevard, and presided over the great comedy boom of the eighties. During the 1980s, The Improv was, as the Visa bankcard television ad used to say, "definitely the place to be." It was packed every night, and celebrities of all stripes used to constantly hang out there. A true character who used to wear a monocle because "it's a nice affectation," Budd was its ubiquitous emcee and impresario, seemingly telling the worst jokes possible before introducing the next act. Though much more youthful-looking than his age of sixty-five, Budd was headed to the Screen Actors Guild to put in for his pension on the day that we did this interview, which was conducted at the Fred Segal restaurant around the corner from The Improv on July 3, 1997.

BUDD FRIEDMAN

How long have you been in the comedy-club business?

I started The Improv in New York in 1960, came out here in 1974, and opened the Los Angeles Improv in 1975.

How many clubs make up The Improv system in total?

We've just opened our ninth club in Miami, and we have a revue called The Improv Extravaganza at the Taj Mahal in Atlantic City in the main room. We've been there for sixteen weeks, and we're gonna take it on the road. We have three comedians who rotate, and we have six singers and dancers who also juggle and tap dance, walk on stilts—they do everything. The whole show is comedy-themed and has been quite successful.

Now the comedy scene is in the midst of a shakeout. Have your clubs survived this shakeout in good shape?

I think the shakeout has finished. The eighties obviously were the highlight of my career and everybody else who was involved in comedy. The early nineties proved to be rather devastating to us. We lost a number of clubs, but the ones that remain are all very solid and very successful. Getting back to the demise of comedy as we know it, I'm sure you're well aware of what happened in the eighties. Everybody and his brother said, if Budd Friedman can make a success of it, I can do it too, and they all opened comedy clubs in restaurants or over a bowling alley. At the same time, guys who should've been accountants or clarinet players became comedians.

So you're saying that there was a lot of mediocrity in comedy that resulted from that boom?

Precisely.

Since the shakeout, do you think that the new comedians you are seeing are getting stronger?

We've lost the fringe guys, and the quality has gone up a little bit because the cream will rise and only the good are going to survive. It is difficult, however, in this day and age to find an individual and original voice because everybody is talking about the same thing.

But can't you still find an original voice in the way that someone approaches a somewhat overused subject?

Absolutely. I remember once when we had a seminar at the club, and L.A. Weekly columinist Judy Brown—who's a very knowledgeable lady with respect to comedy—was sitting on the dais and said, "If I hear one more joke about McDonald's I'll scream." And somebody said, "Oh, really? Did you hear Jay Leno's new routine about McDonald's?" And everyone laughed because they knew that Jay had his own peculiar spin to the day's events, and didn't just take it at face value. Granted, so much in the news today is so humorous that you almost just have to recite it, but it's guys like Jay who can take the news and pervert it for their own uses.

Having started back in the sixties and seventies, you've seen many of the true greats at your clubs. Were there more distinctive voices then?

Back in New York in the sixties, when there was no other comedy clubs or cable comedy shows, every comic we had go on at The Improv you would never, ever confuse with another Improv regular. They were all true individuals. I see a comedy tree that springs from Robert Klein. I think he is definitely at the forefront of the modern stand-up comic.

Most of the comedians I've interviewed felt that Pryor was the best they had ever seen, but most were more influenced by Klein. Why do you think that is?

Klein was more easily assimilated and copied. Pryor had that true comedic genius that is so rare. Robert was funny from the head, and Richard was funny from the heart. When Richard would curse, which was very avant garde in those days, he used words for a purpose. He did not just *Def Comedy Jam* it.

Was Pryor the only comedic genius you've seen?

One of the funniest guys I had on stage was Ron Carey, but Ron just couldn't handle being a stand-up and got into acting. Lily Tomlin would be in that category.

Tell me about your open-mike nights.

Right now, we don't have an open-mike night, and we haven't for a while.

Why not?

It's too painful. Everyone has a videotape these days, so it's much easier to subject me to the indignities of watching these tapes rather than subject an entire audience. And if the tape isn't any good, you can shut it off in a minute or two. If the tape intrigues us, we'll get in touch with them. We've found that most of our acts come through referrals. A comedian might come up to me and say, "Budd, there's a guy who opened up for me that I think that you ought to see," and I'll take a look.

Would someone send you a tape to get work here in L.A. first or at the other clubs?

We'd usually start them out here, then if they do well, we'd move them out to the other clubs.

Apart from the obvious thing of are they funny, what are the things you look at when watching a new comedian?

One of the most important things, of course, is audience response, but I've seen comedians who the audience hasn't laughed at and I'll still encourage them and enjoy them because they have a fresh take and their own voice. I look for originality. I don't want to see someone copying anybody. Also, likeability.

Can likeability compensate for deficient perfoming skills and material?

It's an important factor and it's more important with some people than with others. But we still look for the ability to make people laugh. I was just having this discussion with someone the other day on what's more important, material or delivery? I had to say it's material. Look at Woody Allen. I used to make fun of Joan Rivers' delivery back in New York but one night in my club on stage I did one of her jokes and I died. So I thought, "I guess there is something to her delivery after all."

After over thirty years, are you still the fan of stand-up that you once were when it comes to watching it?

No, but every so often I'll see someone and go, "Uh-huh. That's why I'm still in the business." But I still enjoy going into the club and standing in the back watching the good ones. My wife's a good sport, so no matter where we are, I'll go to a comedy club to check things out, and if we see someone original, we'll go crazy over them.

Can someone be taught to be a good stand-up or is it inbred?

I think that people can teach themselves to be a comedian, but how good they get depends on what's inbred in them. I consider David Brenner a manufactured comedian. He worked his ass off developing his act. He started out going on at five in the morning on 44th Street, he taped every show he ever did, and more importantly, he would go home and listen to the tapes. A lot of comics tape their shows, but don't listen to them. Robert Klein was the first that I know of to use a tape recorder. To show you how far back this was, he had a reel-to-reel Wollensak that he would stick in the back of the room. It was hilarious, when you think about what we use today.

Has it opened up for female comedians? Are you seeing more women come in to try to become comedians?

Not to sound facetious, but there's more of everyone coming into comedy. There's more blacks, there's more Latinos, there's more women, there's more gays who are openly gay. But women were notoriously self-deprecating in their approach to humor in those old days. Some men would be self-deprecating, but not many. Elayne Boosler was one of the first to not do self-deprecating humor. Now I don't see many women being self-deprecating anymore.

Is that a reflection of the feminist movement and them now possessing greater self-esteem?

I don't know if it has anything to do with self-esteem. I think this is what they thought was expected of them, and what the audience would accept. We're talking about the dark ages here.

When did you see that start to change?

I think a lot of that would coincide with the advent of cable and making it accessible to everyone and they could see that self-deprecation wasn't necessary.

Should a comedian try to create an image or let it evolve naturally?

Woody Allen used to be so nervous before he'd perform that he'd throw up. That's his image—so it was natural. We've got a kid from Canada who stands talking with his hand over his mouth. And the first time I saw him, I tried to tell him not to do that, and he told me that it was sort of his trademark. Now it's indispensable. It's become a big part of his act. And I'm sure that it evolved from his own natural nervous tendencies.

Have you ever had a comedian whom you didn't see much potential in really develop and surprise you?

Chris Rock. When Chris first came in, he was an arrogant little snotnose kid, and I took a look and I asked him, "What are you doing, what are you doing?" He came back a year or two later and he was fantastic. I went to him and I said, "You've grown into your arrogance and it works." Before, he'd just been up there on stage blustering, and imitating Eddie Murphy—with no substance. But he worked on his whole being and became a terrific comedian.

Now that there has been a drastic cutback in cable shows and the late-night talk shows don't instantly make stars like ten or fifteen years ago, do the new aspiring comedians have to be prepared for a slower, more gradual road to success?

No, because with the success of stand-ups in sitcoms, on any night, someone can come into the club and see someone who might not have even been on television yet and say, "That's the one we need." We do showcases during pilot season night after night for weeks on end for all the TV people coming in to look for the next Tim Allen or Ellen DeGeneres.

Are there enough new comedians out there with strongly developed ideas and personas who can anchor a sitcom like a Roseanne or Seinfeld? Could getting a show too fast backfire on a weaker-

skilled comedian who doesn't have the power or personal vision to develop a show around themself the way they would like?

That's one of the banes of the existence of network television. They hire a Margaret Cho, who they see in a club doing this wonderful material, and then they put her in a sitcom that has nothing to do with what her act was about. The ones who you mentioned had the balls to say that it was their act, that it was their life, and that it was going to be done their way. I remembered when Roseanne had that run-in with that first producer, everyone said that she was just being a bitch, but you know, the next year the shows were better, and the ratings were better. So Roseanne must've known what she was doing. A friend of mine is managing a young comedian who's terrific and getting a lot of heat. He told me, "I won't let him go near a sitcom now because he's not ready. He can't act." So he's studying acting now to learn what it's all about.

How many young comedians are strong enough to say, Not yet" when the networks offer them an opportunity?

A lot of the wiser managers these days are turning down development deals with networks because they don't want to be tied into what the network wants to do. They want to be able to develop the material with the performer doing the developing. More and more people are waiting now because they know if they get a shot and it doesn't work, they might get another one. Which is smart. I think you have to fight for what you know is right for you.

JAMIE MASADA
(Club Owner, The Laugh Factory)

Jamie Masada is a former comedian from Israel who opened the successful Laugh Factory when he was nineteen years old. A man with a soft spot for comedians and people in general, he is known for his many charitable works in the Hollywood community. A lover of good comedy, he runs an annual Comedy Camp for Kids where students from inner-city schools can learn stand-up comedy from famous practitioners of the art. This interview was conducted at Jamie's office at The Laugh Factory on Sunset Boulevard, on October 4, 1996.

JAMIE MASADA

Jamie, you're from Israel, and you used to be a comedian, right?

Yes, I'm from Israel, and I've been a comedian. I've worked at The Comedy Store.

Did you ever do comedy in Israel?

The comedy I did in Israel was just telling jokes at Bar Mitzvahs and weddings.

Do they have stand-up comedians in Israel in the American sense?

They do stand-up, but it's different in that it's very physical and slapstick.

How long have you been in America?

I came here almost twenty years ago. I worked at the clubs, got a couple TV shows, saved myself some money, then there was a fight going on between the comedians and the comedy-club owners and I felt horrible. So I did some research and I found out this building belonged to Groucho Marx and I leased it.

How old were you when you did this?

I was nineteen.

Did you know what you were doing, or were you just flying by the seat of your pants?

I knew what I was doing because my goal was different.

What was your goal?

My goal came from something my father told me when I was a kid, which was that the greatest mitzvah or greatest good deed you could do for people was to make them laugh. So I used to charge just fifty cents at first, but when I saw people come in with an angry face and then leave with a smile on their face, I felt like the most successful person.

Fifty cents was your rate for everybody?

I started at fifty cents, then a dollar, then two dollars and up.

How long was it before you started noticing that you had regular patrons?

I started having regular patrons right away. I've got people who've been supporting me for seventeen years, people who come sometimes ten times a year.

Did you continue to perform after you started the club?

I performed for the first few years, then I realized that the high that I getting on stage wasn't fair to the other comics. I felt that I was becoming self-indulgent and that to really do good stuff, I had to stop performing.

Since you were able to pull back and stop performing, does that mean that the need to perform was more manageable than many performers whose need to perform drives them?

I just wanted to see people laugh, and it didn't matter whether I made them laugh or someone else made them laugh.

Do you feel that most comedians are neurotic or well-adjusted?

I don't think comics are neurotic. When I did research for my comedy magazine, I found out that comedians have much higher IQs than the average human being.

I don't think neurosis and a high IQ are mutually exclusive.

Some people are nervous or neurotic in real life. That's understandable. But in working with comedians for seventeen years, you can't help but grow to love them because at least ninety percent of them got into the business because they wanted to explore issues close to their hearts. The other ten percent are actors who looked at stand-up as a shortcut to getting a show.

When did you notice that trend start to develop?

I noticed it start right after Eddie Murphy started making money. To be honest, I'm not too fond of those actors who just get into stand-up for that. I can tell right off.

How do you pick up on that?

I can see the motivation. Their motivation is the money, not the love of making people laugh, or the craft of it.

Have you seen any of these actors develop into good stand-up comedians?

Not really. I don't follow their development at all. I only focus on those who are in it for the artistry, and the joy of making people laugh. When I see that true dedication, I try to help. I know that they care, so I try to get them development deals if I can.

Tell me about your open-mike night for amateurs.

I've been holding an open-mike night on Tuesdays for seventeen years, and people have come here from as far as Chicago, Montreal, and Washington, D.C. Some people start camping out on Monday night because only the first twenty people get on. And the reason it's only twenty people is because I give each one a fifteen-minute analysis after they go on, where I go over their material with them and give them feedback on what direction they should go. Some comedians need more than stage time, they need a third eye. I've told some people to stay with their day-time job, because this is the wrong business for them to get into. But I won't tell them that until I've seen them for at least six months.

What has to jump out at you to make you really take notice of a comedian?

I look at their timing, their point of view, their look, their likability, plus their drive—how passionate they are about it. One thing I hate is a comedian who get laughs at other people's expense. Other clubs allow that, but I don't. I'm very passionate about the comedian's material. If someone comes in and does somebody else's material that is proven, I say okay, the first six months they are trying to learn, but after six months if they aren't writing their own material, I say, "Don't come back in here." I encourage the young comedians to write their own material. I tell them when they are out doing their daily stuff, always look at a way to find something funny in what's going on. Just try. This way the mind gets trained. You'd be surprised, but after six months of that, any person could start writing jokes.

Do you find many fully formed comedians at an early stage? Most of the comedians I talked to say they bombed for at least a year.

I've seen people bomb for two or three years. That's no problem because you see in that particular person the drive, timing, or a lot of other stuff going for them. I'll still encourage them.

How have you seen comedy change in the last seventeen years?

There was a lot of shock-value humor out years ago, but that's shaken out, and now there's a return to good intelligent comedy again.

IRVIN ARTHUR

(Talent Agent)

Irvin Arthur of Irvin Arthur & Associates has been a talent agent for over forty years. A gentle man with a love of artists and a sharp eye for talent, Irvin was the talent booker for the old Playboy Club and gave me my first two-week job at the San Francisco Playboys Club. (I was fired in a week.) He's represented many of the great comedic artists during his career, including Steve Allen, Bette Midler, Lily Tomlin, and Richard Pryor. He still retains the zest and enthusiasm for the business of someone just starting out. He was kind enough to come speak to my class in the summer of 1992.

IRVIN ARTHUR

How did you get into being an agent?

I had been an actor when I was young in New York, making the rounds and stuff like that. Also, I was in legitimate theater, directing summer stock, when I just reached a moment of truth where I realized that I didn't have "it." In a freak accident, I walked into my agent's office forty years ago and while she was on the phone, the other phone rang and she said, "Irvin, grab the phone." So I picked up the phone and some guy from a bar called The Lighthouse on Broadway and 74th Street said, "Hey, I'm looking for an organist." And with no idea of what I was talking about, I said, "I've got one for you." Then I turned to my agent and said, "This guy's looking for an organist," and she handed me an American Federation of Musicians book that listed musicians by instrument. I looked under organists and saw a guy named Don Evans (who I'd never seen before or since), and I told the guy on the phone that I had a terrific organist named Don Evans for him. The guy said, "I need him for four weeks." I said, "That'll be $250 a week." The guy said, "Can he start tonight?" I told him I'd call him and let him know. Then I called Don Evans and told him that I was an agent with a job and would he pay me ten percent commission? He said, "No problem." Then I turned to my agent and said, "Hey, I like this." And that's how it happened.

What exactly does an agent do?

An agent is really an employment agent. He or she goes out and finds talent that they believe that they can find work for. Sometimes you find people at the embryonic stage of their career, and you hope that you can grow with them as they develop. I've been very lucky. I have this knack of being able to tell early on with people that there's some talent there. In New York I signed people like Woody Allen, Bette Midler, Lily Tomlin, David Steinberg, Kenny Rogers and The First Edition, and Barbra Streisand. And many times I've been wrong. One of my secretaries in New York was a little blond lady named Joan Rivers, who I never believed would make it, but she had this perseverance that went beyond the limit. I would go and see her at a little club called The Duplex. She'd use some of Woody Allen's material, some of Henny Youngman's, she didn't care. She was very democratic. Woody Allen's manager, Jack Rollins, would call me, and she would do five minutes on the phone, then turn to me and say, "By the way, Jack Rollins is on the phone." She was just so determined. She'd made a commitment.

When you work, do you call the clubs or do they call you?

Both. Most of the time we're calling them if we've got someone new who we're trying to get that first break. It certainly helps to represent people who are well known. People are calling you for them, and then we use that as a wedge to get the unknown person a job.

When you look at a comedian in an embryonic stage, what are some of the things you look for?

You look for a likability, a stage presence, and you look for some kind of an intelligence in that there's a beginning, middle, and end, or a potential for a beginning, middle, and end to a piece of a material that a person is doing. You look for that natural funniness. There used to be a time, more so years ago than now, when comedians would be very funny off stage. They just couldn't help it. Now there is more of a dual personality in comedians. When they're on stage, they're working at their craft, molding and shaping material. But off the stage they're very, very serious—like an actor. So it's always been interesting to me to find that person off stage who has a funniness about them.

In the embryonic stage, should a comedian do a lot of open-mike nights at clubs?

Definitely. And always be compelled to do the best you can on any given night. That's part of the discipline. Don't ever throw a performing opportunity away. I can't emphasize that enough. You've got that five minutes on stage, and believe me, you won't know who's in the audience. I get calls from all the owners of the clubs in the city saying that I've got to come and see a new comedian. It happens all the time, and either I will go or one of the people in my office will go see them.

When you see someone new, how closely do you evaluate their material?

For me it all melds together. When the material gels and the person delivers it well, then you've found yourself someone special. However, in the beginning you're looking for someone who has the stage presence to attract attention from the audience, and compel it to watch them. I firmly believe that it's the persona first, and then the material. Even though the person may not know how to dress on stage, how to hold a microphone, or even the proper choice of words, there is something about their personality that allows an effective communication between themselves on stage and the audience. The interesting thing about Woody Allen when I saw him at his first job at The Bitter End was how nervous he was on stage. He was so nervous that he twisted the mike cord and stalked the stage. Yet it worked for him. Some people it doesn't work for.

Can you tell if someone has potential from watching only five minutes of material?

I can only tell if I like them or not, and whether I want to see them again.

With the huge number of comedians out there now, is it easier or harder for a young comedian to distinguish him or herself from the pack?

I don't think that the number of comedians out there makes it more difficult to get to that gem—that person with the gold.

Is there any particular method that a beginning comedian can use to develop and improve?

The most important thing that a new stand-up can do is just work, work, work all the time. Go on wherever you can go on. You should tape-record every performance. You have to treat your craft as a business. And have a lot of discipline. I don't know anything tougher than being a stand-up comedian. I don't know any other performer who gets up in front of strangers and pours out their heart and soul. It's quite a chore to do that every night, and it just boggles the mind that you have to be able to have the ability to accept that challenge.

Can you talk a little bit about the artist-to-agent introduction process?

The first thing to remember is that the agent is looking for you. If you have talent, we want you as bad as you want us. It's how we make our living. It's how we get our kicks. As agents, we're looking for—and I'm sure it's an overused word—but we're looking for "magic." And if you believe you have it, then find out which agents represent your favorite comedians—because you want whomever is representing that kind of artist to represent you. Then you just seek them out.

When you find a person who you think has "it" but is very raw, how do you go about creating the agent-client relationship?

You watch them for a while, or you may have a handshake agreement with them that you'll get them jobs, and you'll go out and see them. Then when they reach a certain level of development, you tie the knot, so to speak.

When you say "tie the knot," does that mean that a contract is entered into?

Yes. In personal appearances we have a contract called a General Services Agreement, which is for one, two, or three years. I have a theory that when you're signing someone who is young and inexperienced to never sign them for less than a three-year period. The reason being that there is an awful lot of time and money invested in trying to secure work for them. If not, it becomes a revolving door. By the way, this agreement is drawn up by the state employment commission and is designed to protect the artist.

What is the best protocol for a client in dealing with an agent if they are having a problem getting bookings?

The best approach is a confrontation between the agent and the client where the two of you sit down and the client asks, "Why aren't you getting me work? What seems to be the problem?" And the agent has to be straight with the client and state exactly what the problem is. There could be any number of reasons. Maybe the client has a reputation for difficulty. Or maybe he or she just doesn't draw enough customers. That's why it's tough for a new act to get an agent.

Is there any difference between an agent and manager?

Yes. A very distinct difference. An agent is licensed by the state that he has his office in as an employment agency. There are a lot of restrictions, including one that you can't have a couch or a sofa in your office. Because of the infamous "casting couch," they've made that part of the law. Also, the maximum amount of commission that an agent can get is ten percent. With a manager, the sky is the limit. Whatever deal you make with a manager is valid. I've known some managers to get fifty percent, and some of them are still managing that client. What they do is form a partnership with all the expenses coming off the top, then the manager and the artist share what's left after the expenses that they both incur. But I'd say the average fee for a manager is fifteen percent.

What's the relationship between a manager and an agent?

Usually the manager is responsible for selecting the agent for the client. It is literally against the law for the manager to solicit work, so when an agent has an offer to make to a client, he calls the personal manager and presents the offer to him. They discuss the offer together and decide if it's a good move for the client. Another difference between manager and agents is that agents have many clients, while managers have only a few. Thus there is usually a closer tie between a manager and client than there is between agent and client. The managers whom I know have a genuine, caring commitment to their clients.

Some people feel that the easy availability of comedy on television has definitely cut into the attendance at comedy clubs. Is that true?

I think the saturation on television has had some effect that way.

How do you assess the health of the comedy-club scene around the country since a number of comedy clubs seem to be closing?

I think it's gonna be survival of the fittest. There are some clubs in soft markets in economically depressed areas, but on the weekends these clubs are holding up in big cities. The clubs that are going to survive are going to be those that have a good sense of marketing and know how to run their establishments. I hear that clubs are having tough times, but I don't see it. I find that we're able to come up with work for people.

BUDDY MORRA
(Personal Manager)

Buddy Morra is a partner in Morra, Brezner, Steinberg, one of the entertainment industry's top personal-management companies. A laid-back, extremely soft-spoken, and casual man, Buddy and his company have specialized in comedic performers over the years, managing to great success such stars as Billy Crystal, Robin Williams, David Letterman, Paula Poundstone, Kathy Griffin, Jake Johansen, and Robert Klein—all of whom started out as stand-up comedians. This interview was conducted at a restaurant near his West L.A. office in July of 1996.

BUDDY MORRA

Is it tougher finding comedic talent that interests you nowadays?

I don't go to the clubs nearly as much as I used to. I still pop in here and there. I go to the Montreal and Aspen comedy festivals, but I haven't seen much that's knocked me out. It gets a little disheartening, because really it's a wonderful profession. Being a stand-up comedian is a very special thing. It's the hardest single thing to do in entertainment, and doing it right is even harder.

I've heard many people in the entertainment industry say stand-up's the hardest. Why do you think it's the hardest art form?

Because it requires thought, it requires timing, it requires attention. Say you're a singer in Vegas, and the audience is having dinner. The audience doesn't have to pay attention to the singer because the minute the song is over the band hits a chord, and the audience knows it's time to look up and applaud. A comedian doesn't have that luxury. He's gotta be funny. He's gotta make them laugh, because if they don't laugh, then you're not succeeding. And in order to make them laugh, you have to have their full attention.

As a long-time manager of stand-up comedians, what do you see that's different with today's stand-up comedians?

Nobody works on their act anymore. All they want to do is get together six minutes to do *The Tonight Show*.

They're not looking to develop forty-five minutes to an hour like past generations?

No. I know that with the clients we've had through the years, before we put them on *The Tonight Show*, we always made sure that they had at least three shots' worth of good material. So if the first one went as well as it should go, then when they went back three weeks later, the next one was as good or better, and then the third one was as good or better. Then you could create some momentum, some heat. No one has three shots these days. All they want to do is get one six-minute hunk together and they think the world's gonna change. And it's not gonna change because they're not doing individual stuff. It's very imitative. You could take the material of ninety percent of the comedians out there and give it to someone else and it would be the same.

So you feel that point of view is lacking?

Point of view, attitude. When I first saw Letterman, who was never the strongest stand-up comedian, you saw an attitude, a point of view—whether you liked it or not. There was something unique and special about him. Nowadays there is very little unique and special about most of the people out there. Now, by the way, they want a series right away.

How did that mentality take hold?

Once a few comedians made the successful transition to being in a series, that made everyone want to do it. So the new ones didn't have to work as hard to get better as comedians, because all they wanted was a series. Some of them could act, and some of them couldn't. What happened ten years ago with the explosion of comedy, is that the demand exceeded the supply. So you were seeing an incredible number of mediocre comedians with little interest in the craft.

So they weren't trying to develop as stand-up comedians but looking at being a comedian only as a short-cut to television?

If you look at the comedians from Jack Benny, George Burns to Newhart, Cosby, Seinfeld, Roseanne, by the time they did a series, they had done stand-up long enough to really learn about comedy. They knew performing. Now everybody comes out, "How ya doing, where you from?" Who cares? They're not trying to develop. Someone once said to me that most performers spend most of their time waiting for the opportunity, instead of preparing for it. If you prepare for the opportunity, and you have the ability, the opportunity will come.

It seems that *The Tonight Show* and *Letterman* are not the launching ground for comedians that they used to be.

That's very true. In the old days, everyone worked hard to get *The Tonight Show*, and when you got it, it meant something when you did well. People got hot off of those shows. Not anymore. Today it's just an appearance.

When you talk to the younger comedians, do you find them resistant or receptive to your ideas in that area?

I usually don't go around offering my advice—it's not my place to do that, except to my own clients. But if someone comes over and asks me for some advice, I'll be happy to talk to them and tell them what I think.

At what stage do you like to get involved in a client's career? At the early stage or after they're more developed?

We much prefer being there from day one. And pretty much all of our relationships with our clients have been that way. We've had Billy Crystal from day one, we've had Robin Williams from day one. We like to give them our thoughts, our input. We get off creatively that way too. It's a longer process doing it that way for us in terms of making money, but we've always believed if the quality is there, it may be a little slower, but it'll be there a long time when it hits.

What catches your attention when you're interested in someone? Do you look at their material?

Material is almost incidental. Someone once said years ago, "When the audience walks out, do they remember the joke, or do they remember the person?" If they remember the joke, you're in trouble. We're just starting to work with a young lady, Kathy Griffin [who was later a supporting actor on NBC's *Suddenly Susan*], who is doing very non-traditional comedy. She doesn't do boyfriend jokes, she doesn't do mother-in-law stuff. She talks about what happened to her and it's all true, though she's extended it to make it funnier. She has an individual point of view, and you can't take what she does and give it to someone else because it won't work. When you see her, you know there's something unique and special about her right off the bat. That's what we look for anyway.

Point of view is a way of looking at life, and all of us have one, right?

But not all of us can express it, or at least express it on stage so that it becomes funny.

Are some people afraid to put their point of view on stage?

Absolutely. But I've always believed that in order to be a really wonderful performer, certainly in comedy, it's almost like analysis. You have to strip yourself. That's the only way it can work. Because if you pull back, then the audience will pull back.

How is that manager-client relationship initiated? Do you approach people or do they come to you?

Both ways. The first time I saw Letterman, I was knocked out and I found out he was handled by somebody. So I didn't approach him then, but later when I found out he was no longer being handled by anybody, I went over to him and said I thought he was terrific and I'd like to talk to him. He came by a few days later and we got together. Sometimes club owners call us and recommend acts to us to check out. Which we'll do.

How do you take a young comedian who can write and has a point of view and build a career, assuming that they are receptive to your input?

They're all agreeable to our input in the beginning, because simply it comes down to the fact that they need us more than we need them. We try and take their special voice and find the right vehicle for it.

Are you always successful at that?

Not all the time. For example, we had Paula Poundstone for about ten years. We don't have Paula anymore, which is something I've always regretted because I happen to think she's just incredibly talented. She's a very special voice. We could never find the key to make it happen for her. We tried everything. We got her five shows at HBO to do as a possible series. That didn't work. She left after ten years, and again I was very sorry to see her go. She is an original. Sometimes a person can be so talented and unique that there is no place for them.

By that you mean on a mass-acceptance level, but not in terms of building a niche?

Right. A niche she's got. But we couldn't take her to the highest level.

Do they all want to go to the highest level or are some comfortable with just finding a niche?

I think everybody wants to get to that highest level. I think they will settle for a niche once they've made that attempt and not succeeded.

As your relationship develops with a client over time, are they more or less resistant to sitting with you after shows and letting you break down and analyze their act?

It varies. After all, they come to us because we have a reputation of being successful with acts, and they're hoping we'll be successful with them. So they do listen. They have their own voice, and sometimes they disagree, which is fine. We're good at what we do, but none of us is a genius. We make mistakes. If they feel real strongly about something, we'll say, "All right, try it and let's see how it works." If it works, cool; if not, we'll suggest they try it another way.

Can a client be too difficult for you to handle despite the fact that they're very talented?

Absolutely.

Would it be temperament, volatility, or stubbornness?

Probably a combination of all of those things. We've been fortunate in that our clients for the most part have truly been nice people who we work well with and have good relationships. Certainly we've disagreed with them at times and have had arguments, but basically we don't make decisions for our clients. We bring them anything that's legitimate, tell them what we think, and then they make the decision. We may disagree with their decision, but many times they've been right and we've been wrong. But we've been right more times than wrong.

Do you think every comedian needs a manager?

No. I don't think they're a necessity, but I think they can be very helpful and important to different people at certain times in their life.

Should someone get a manager before they get an agent or vice versa?

That's kind of like, What's first, the chicken or the egg? Particularly the way we work because we like to start with a client from day one. Agents don't like to work with people at the start. They like them to be at a certain level before they jump in. So at certain times we have to act as an agent to get our comedians jobs. Even back when we had Klein and he was with William Morris, I used to call the colleges myself to book him, 'cause they didn't have a college department. Now you're not supposed to do that, but you do what you have to do to keep the client alive and working.

Since you have to spend a lot of time with a client, does an emotional connection develop?

It's hard for me not to be emotionally involved. It started back with Jo Anne Worley when I'd be on the side of the stage and she'd be going out on *Merv Griffin*. My armpits would just be dripping wet. It's like they're an extension of you.

Do some clients need a lot of emotional support?

Some need it and want it, and some don't want it.

Have your splits with your clients usually been amicable?

It's always been an amicable situation except on one occasion with a comedian who was not a big name, but was getting there, who came and left. We had gotten him a lot of exposure, and he just left. That bothered me. It happens. It's part of the industry. But the interesting thing with our company is that when somebody leaves, for some strange reason, a week, two weeks, a month later, someone interesting comes in to replace them.

FRANKLYN AJAYE

Franklyn Ajaye is an Emmy-nominated writer/producer/actor/comedian. Among his many television writing and producing credits are *The Parent'Hood, In Living Color, Roc, NYPD Blue*, and *Politically Incorrect*. Among his acting credits are *Carwash, Hollywood Shuffle, The Burbs*, and *Stir Crazy*. As a noted comedian, he has appeared *on The Tonight Show, Politically Incorrect, The David Letterman Show*, and *The Arsenio Hall Show* and has worked everywhere from small clubs to the major Las Vegas hotels, as well as the Melbourne International Comedy Festival and the Edinburgh Fringe Festival. In addition, he has had three recordings of his comedy work released by A&M and Little David Records and has taught stand-up comedy at UCLA. Known internationally as "The Jazzcomedian," Franklyn now splits his time between Los Angeles, California, and Melbourne, Australia, where he teaches television writing, plays clarinet, and performs with his musician brother Eric in comedy and music festivals.